# ARTSPRAXIS
*Emphasizing critical analysis of the arts in society.*

ISSN: 1552-5236

EDITOR
**Jonathan P. Jones**, *New York University, USA*

EDITORIAL BOARD
**Amanda Brown**, *East Carolina University, USA*
**Selina Busby**, *The Royal Central School of Speech and Drama, UK*
**Manjima Chatterjee**, *Shiv Nadar School, India*
**Durell Cooper**, *Cultural Innovation Group, USA*
**Rivka Eckert**, *State University of New York at Potsdam, USA*
**Rosalind M. Flynn**, *The Catholic University of America, USA*
**Kelly Freebody**, *The University of Sydney, Australia*
**Anna Glarin**, *York St John University, UK*
**Courtney Grile**, *Savannah College of Art and Design, USA*
**Norifumi Hida**, *Tsubouchi Memorial Theatre Museum, Waseda University, Japan*
**Byoung-joo Kim**, *Seoul National University of Education, South Korea*
**Gillian McNally**, *University of Northern Colorado, USA*
**David Montgomery**, *New York University, USA*
**Ross Prior**, *University of Wolverhampton, UK*
**Amanda Rutter**, *The University of Texas Permian Basin, USA*
**Sara Schroeter**, *University of Regina, Canada*
**Nkululeko Sibanda**, *Rhodes University, South Africa*
**Daphnie Sicre**, *Loyola Marymount University, USA*
**Tammie Swopes**, *New York University, USA*
**Amanda Wager**, *Vancouver Island University, Canada*
**James Webb**, *Davidson College, USA*
**Gustave Weltsek**, *Indiana University Bloomington, USA*
**Petronilla Whitfield**, *Arts University Bournemouth, UK*

ArtsPraxis Volume 11, Issue 1 looked to engage members of the global Educational Theatre community in dialogue around current research and practice. We welcomed traditional academic research as well as narratives of practice. The call for papers was released in concert with the publication of ArtsPraxis Volume 10, Issue 2. The submission deadline for Volume 11, Issue 1 was **March 1, 2024.**

Submissions fell under one of the following categories:
- Drama in Education (i.e., studies in drama/theatre curriculum, special education, integrated arts, assessment and evaluation)
- Applied Theatre (i.e., studies in community-based theatre, theatre of the oppressed, the teaching artist, diversity and inclusion)
- Theatre for Young Audiences and Youth Theatre (i.e., studies in acting, directing,

dramaturgy, playwriting, dramatic literature, theatre technology, arts-based research methodologies)

Article submissions addressed the following questions:

Drama in Education
- How and why do we teach drama and theatre in schools and community settings?
- How do the roles and responsibilities of the teaching artist differ from those of the classroom teacher (primary, secondary or higher education)?
- What is the contemporary role of drama and theatre in arts education?
- How do we prepare future theatre artists and educators in the 21st century?
- What are innovative ways of devising original works and/or teaching theatre using various aesthetic forms, media, and/or technology?
- To what extent can the study of global theatre forms impact students' learning?
- To what extent should we distinguish theatre-making from drama as a learning medium?
- How can integrated-arts curricula facilitate teaching, learning and presenting the craft of theatre?
- How do we assess students' aesthetic understanding and awareness?
- What research supports the potential of drama as a learning medium?
- How do drama and theatre make connections across curricular content areas and beyond schools?
- How do drama and theatre education contribute to lifelong learning?
- What role do drama and theatre play in community agencies?

Applied Theatre
- How can drama provide a forum to explore ideas?
- What are innovative strategies for using drama to stimulate dialogue, interaction and change?
- How is theatre being used to rehabilitate people in prisons, health facilities, and elsewhere?
- How do we prepare future artists/educators for work in applied theatre?
- What ethical questions should the artist/educator consider in their work?
- In what ways are aesthetics important in applied theatre? How do we negotiate a commitment to both the process and product of applied theatre work?
- How do artist/educators assess participants' understandings in an applied theatre project?
- What are the major tensions in the field and how are these being addressed?
- To what extent has recent research on affect influenced community-based praxis?

Theatre for Young Audiences/Youth Theatre
- Theatre for young audiences is an international movement and the borders are breaking down so how do we present and respond to work from other countries?
- Who exactly are our new audiences—who are we talking to?
- Are we as brave as we think we are? How does what we think we should do relate to what we want to do as artists?
- Is the writer at the heart of future theatre creation? What has happened to dramaturgy in the brave new world of immersive, experiential, visual/physical theatre?
- Theatre for Young Audiences has always been in the forefront of theatrical innovation.

- So what is next?
- What have we learned about nurturing the artist of the future-- playwriting, theatre-making, performance?
- How do artists establish rigorous, intentional new works development processes that are innovative and sustainable?
- How does accountability serve the stakeholders in a new works development process?
- How do we define and measure success in theatre for young audiences?

We encouraged article submissions from interdisciplinary artists, educators, and scholars. Our goal was to motivate a dialogue among a wide variety of practitioners and researchers that will enrich the development of educational theatre in the coming years.

Call for Papers
Papers were to be no longer than 6,000 words, had to be accompanied by a 200 word abstract and 100 word biographies for the author(s), and conformed to APA style manual. For this issue, articles could include traditional academic scholarship and narratives of practice.

Reviewing Procedures
Each article was sent to two peer reviewers. They provided advice on the following:
- Whether the article should be published with no revisions/with revisions.
- The contribution the article makes to the arts community.
- Specific recommendations to the author about improving the article.
- Other publishing outlets if the article is considered unacceptable.

Editorial correspondence should be addressed to [Jonathan P. Jones](mailto:jonathan.jones@nyu.edu), New York University, Program in Educational Theatre, Pless Hall, 82 Washington Square East, Rm 223, New York, NY 10003, USA. Email: jonathan.jones@nyu.edu

Cover image from NYU Steinhardt / Program in Educational Theatre / New Plays for Young Audiences at the Provincetown Playhouse in 2024 by Teresa Fisher.

© 2024 New York University

# ARTSPRAXIS

Volume 11    Issue 1    June 2024

**Editorial: E Pluribus Unum**  i
Jonathan P. Jones

**A Collective Vision for a Future in the Arts through Community and Civic Engagement Programs**  1
Sharon Counts

**"We Can Help!": Using Creative Drama to Explore Social Justice in Youth Theatre**  14
Maddie N. Zdeblick and Noëlle GM Gibbs

**'If they can't come to you, go to them': Pivot-Spaces and Kinesthetic Spectatorship in Back Alley Parade Performances for Young Audiences**  39
James Woodhams

**Pedagogy, Practice, and Performance: A Practical and Phenomenological Approach with Long Island Classics Stage Company's Classic Kids**  64
David Overton

**Enhancing Critical Thinking Skills and Ethical Responsibility in UK Higher Education in Times of "Polycrisis": Two Case Studies from Drama and Theatre Arts**  83
Ellen Redling

**Social Justice and Fringe Theatre in Higher Education**  106
Dermot Daly

**Re*imagining* Learning Spaces: The Rise of Theatrical Inquiry in Arts Education**  121
Nicholas Waxman

**Praxis: The Application of Teaching and Deep Learning Strategies for the DBI Education Practitioner/Researcher**  140
Brenda Burton

ArtsPraxis
Volume 11 Issue 1
© 2024

# Editorial: E Pluribus Unum

## JONATHAN P. JONES
NEW YORK UNIVERSITY

I'm so happy to know that flag flying is back in style. The horror across the way from the building where my office is located makes me want to fly a flag outside. The flag would be emblazoned with only one word: Shame. This way, anyone standing outside of Gould Plaza here at NYU would know how I feel. And they'd likely be outside of Gould Plaza rather than *on* the plaza as this hideous wall of shame (Figure 1) prevents access and blights the landscape. To be blunt: if you're arresting your students for peaceful protest, you're doing it wrong.

When we saw film of the students at Columbia University who barricaded themselves inside a building and were damaging property to protest is support of Gaza—at least you could make a case about public safety. But when NYU brought in the police to arrest protestors at the Gaza Solidarity Encampment, the situation was quite different.

"In the May 1 memo, [NYU President] Mills wrote that only 65 of the 133 individuals arrested at the plaza were affiliated with the university" (Nehme, 2024). *Only*? "Mills stated that hundreds of demonstrators on campus last Monday 'did not have permission to be

**Figure 1:** The wall of shame—a wooden wall constructed around Gould Plaza at NYU. Photo by the author.

at NYU' and 'significantly threatened' the university community" (Nehme, 2024). As one of my students said, "A protest that doesn't disrupt anything is just a gathering of friends." And at NYU where most classes happen during the day, what of a protest outside a building complex that has multiple entries and exits after normal class hours—and certainly after office hours—when the buildings are largely vacant? *What were they disrupting? What were they threatening?* The wall was erected the day after, and as of this writing, it is now more than six weeks since these events unfolded, and the wall remains.

Another student said, "But they were chanting they supported Hamas." To which I replied with some version of this:

> We do have freedom of speech in this country. And even if the speech is hate speech, it is protected speech. I don't agree with it. I don't like it. But an academic institution is supposed to be invested in the development of student voice and choice, not the arbiter of what political speech they will tolerate. And while I know that some feel that hate speech makes them feel threatened and unsafe—to be clear, standing up New York City Police outside of every campus building and in and around Washington Square is a live threat. ANYTHING could happen, be that a real act or a perceived act, and no one would be safe from the police response.

My heart was pounding in my chest. The day after the wall was erected, I had back-to-back classes that evening in two different buildings (identified as '1' and '2' in Figure 2).

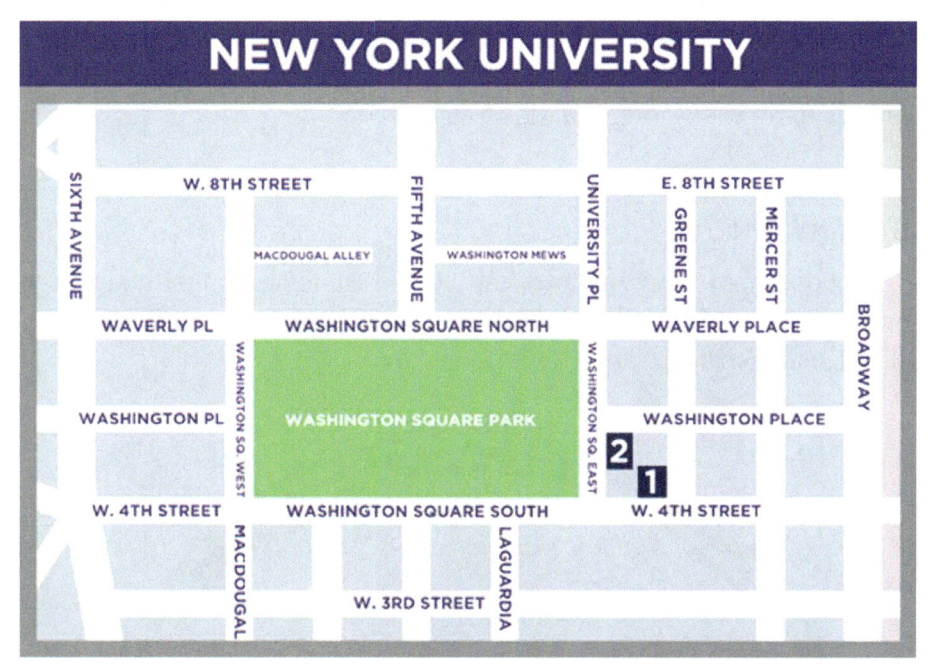

**Figure 2:** A map of NYU's Washington Square campus indicating author's class locations

The 'encampment' had relocated a few blocks south and there was a protest march heading southbound on Mercer Street, two blocks away. As I made my way around the corner (from '1' on the map) to get to the second class building ('2' on the map), there were police stationed everywhere. A student and I observed what appeared to be a bloodied protester being carried by a cadre of police officers along Washington Square East. I had been following the unfolding horrors in Israel and Gaza for seven months and stayed silent about it in my classes. *What was there to say?* But arresting students for protesting the university's investment was a bridge too far. Particularly given the outcry from right wing politicians that universities and colleges were not doing enough to quell the political speech of their students. *Yes, let's set the scene to reimagine Kent State for a new generation.*[1] And so I spoke up. But I

---

[1] "On May 4, 1970, members of the Ohio National Guard fired into a crowd of Kent State University demonstrators, killing four and wounding nine Kent State (cont.)

Editorial: E Pluribus Unum

must reflect on the fact that the same fear is what kept me silent for all those months. That same fear is what instigated my tame comment in the last editorial for this publication, "That seemingly unlimited arms support will be given in furtherance of a humanitarian disaster" (Jones, 2023, vii)—milquetoast, at best. And I agonized over every word in that sentence. That's what 'they' want. They want us to be careful. They want us to be silent. And that has to stop.

**OF MANY, ONE**

E pluribus unum. This motto of the United States was first suggested by a committee on July 4, 1776, and now appears on the country's official seal (Smithsonian Institute).

**Figure 3:** The Great Seal of the United States (US Department of State, 2018)

---

students" (Lewis and Hensley, 1998). The students were protesting the expanding war in Vietnam, as the US invaded neighboring Cambodia.

And the motto has many layers of meaning. On one hand, it speaks to the federal system of disparate states conjoined under one federal government. On the other, it highlights this country as constituted largely of immigrant populations. And underpinning all of this is a diversity of perspectives, persuasions, cultures, and beliefs—united in one common cause. A democratic system that is designed to balance popular sentiment with protections for minority groups. And yet, we sort ourselves—divide ourselves politically in ways that sometimes seem to defy logic.

Below, I detail the most important issues facing the US as identified by tracking polls of US voters by *YouGov* (2024). The descriptions are my own.

### *Inflation/Prices*

Following the COVID-19 pandemic, the economies across the Global North have struggled through work stoppages, supply-chain disruption, and global inflation. Here in the US, the public rates this highest among their political concerns—as if to say, "we want the government to control prices!" But that's not the economic system we have here. The government does not control the price of goods—these are set by 'market forces.' Supply and demand, if you will. Or price-gouging, if you know (FTC, 2024). No matter. The liberal viewpoint seeks to reign in business in so far as the capitalist system will allow (though limited, not impossible). The conservative viewpoint is to let the market sort it out.

And yet, with a comparatively low inflation rate (as compared to other economies in the Global North), expanding GDP, and low unemployment, a *Wall Street Journal* survey of economists describes the US economy as "the envy of the world" (Goldfarb and DeBarros, 2024). While comparatively enviable, the cost of housing, food, goods, and services are too high—and yet, we consume and blame politicians for something that, in the system as currently constituted, is largely beyond their control.

### Jobs and the Economy

For all my life, public polling shows that the US public trusts the Republican party more than the Democratic party when it comes to the economy. And yet, job growth has been larger under Democratic administrations (*The Economist*, 2024). The same is true for GDP growth—on average, better under Democratic administrations (Bivens, 2024). True for decades. And yet, *we believe.*

### Immigration

According to Pew Research, "about three-quarters of Americans (73%) say increasing security along the U.S.-Mexico border to reduce illegal crossings should be a [...] goal for US immigration policy" (Oliphant and Cerda, 2022). Beyond that unified vision, the liberal viewpoint seeks to provide a path to citizenship for undocumented immigrants and expand access to the Deferred Action for Childhood Arrivals (DACA) program. The conservative viewpoint is mass deportation. And yet, there has been no meaningful immigration reform for nearly four decades.

### Taxes and Government Spending

We want to pay no taxes. And we want roads, and bridges, and street lights, and police, and schools, and national parks, and prisons, and social security, and Medicare, and on and on and on. What we want is to end corruption. What we want is to stop waste. Last fall, in response to this litany, a student said, "What I want is to not have all of our money going to support the military industrial complex." Touché. The liberal viewpoint seeks to make the wealthy and corporations pay their fair share. Tax and spend, some might say. The conservative viewpoint is to cut taxes for the wealthy and corporations. Starve the beast and prioritize privatization.

### Climate Change

The liberal viewpoint seeks to expand access to renewable energy sources and support industrial innovation. The conservative viewpoint is ...

Elsewhere in the Global North, politicians debate how to confront (arguably) the single largest problem facing humanity. And in the US, it's a hoax. It's a natural phenomenon and we have no control over it. It's a global problem; why should our economy suffer when India and China…

**The Supreme Court**

…

I've been teaching public speaking for over a decade, and at the end of each semester, I impart some version of this guidance to students:

> I don't care what side of the issues you find yourself, but there is NO QUESTION that the political parties have a different opinion on most of them. And in this imperfect system—this federation—our most vital act of speaking publicly is to vote. When chicken and fish are the options, you choose. And if your legal status is such that you can't choose, then you find people who can choose and you get them to the polls. And if you don't want chicken or fish, then you must step up and run for office yourself.

As American as apple pie is the notion that politicians are all the same. Political contests are often characterized as the lesser of two evils. The menu needs to be reimagined. But until then, chicken or fish are the options.

I am steeped in politics every day. And the behavior of politicians does not phase me. Some are desperate to better society. Others are out to make a buck. Charlatans abound. They don't phase me as they are artifacts of society at large, as they should be. What really gets at me is *us*. The voters. The ill-informed. The low-information voters. The tribalists. In October 2008, I was with a group of friends waiting at a pedestrian crossing when one said, "How many times do you have to hear that someone is a Muslim before you start to believe it?" I turned to her and said, "They can say it as many times as they want. It doesn't make it true. And even if it was true, what difference would that make?"

We must be informed. We must decipher the credibility of our sources. We must confront distrust and disengagement. As educators and artists, we have the tools—so we must spread the word.

As I highlighted at the outset of this editorial, there is a vested interest in promoting cynicism. To feel powerless. That there is nothing to be done. That if we speak up, they will shut us down. That both sides are the same and nothing changes. And yet I remind you that in 2017, control of the Virginia House of Delegates literally came down to a coin toss (Bump, 2017). Every vote matters.

And you don't need to digest politics on the regular. In an appearance on *The Michelangelo Signorile Show* in early May 2024, Mark Joseph Stern, senior writer for *Slate* on the courts and the law, paraphrased a tweet he'd authored a few years ago: "The supreme court has already ruined the country; that doesn't mean they should ruin your weekend too."

> **Mark Joseph Stern**
> @mjs_DC
>
> My line on this is that the Supreme Court is already ruining the country; you shouldn't let it ruin your vacation too. Have a blast and delete this app!
>
> 9:59 AM · Aug 25, 2021

**Figure 4:** Mark Joseph Stern's August 25, 2021 tweet

Of many, one. We are all entitled to a weekend or vacation from politics, but we must engage. Choose your flag—rest assured that Martha-Ann Alito will choose hers (I'll leave you to find your own source)—and fly that flag. There's too much at stake.

**IN THIS ISSUE**

In this issue, our contributors document and reflect on innovative educational theatre practices for youth theatre and theatre for young audiences, in higher education, and research methodologies. **Sharon Counts** advocates for civic and community engagement programs as one prominent and effective method to foster synergy between communities and arts organizations. **Maddie N. Zdeblick** and **Noëlle GM Gibbs** investigate their dynamic use of creative drama to explore social justice in youth theatre. **James Woodhams** analyzes Back Alley Puppetry Parade performances during the COVID-19 pandemic to document pivot-spaces and kinesthetic spectatorship. **David Overton** shares a heuristic and phenomenological self-study about the Long Island Classics Stage Company. On the higher education front, **Ellen Redling** proposes methods for enhancing critical thinking skills and ethical responsibility as revealed through two case studies. **Dermot Daly** uses a similar methodical approach, examining social justice and fringe theatre in higher education. Finally, **Nicholas Waxman** deconstructs the rise of theatrical inquiry as a research methodology in arts education, and **Brenda Burton** presents a literature review on the application of teaching and deep learning strategies for the drama-based instruction (DBI) practitioner and researcher.

**LOOKING AHEAD**

As we have recently concluded another thought-provoking dialogue at Amplify & Ignite, the 2024 Symposium on Research and Scholarship (presented in concert with the American Alliance for Theatre & Education/AATE), our next issue (Volume 11, Issue 2) will focus on articles that respond to or demonstrate a reimaging of research and scholarship in educational theatre. We invite submissions that will fall under one of the following frames:

- Researcher as artist
- Researcher as audience member
- Researcher as educator
- Expansive understandings of research and scholarship from emerging and seasoned scholars
- Decolonized and antiracist research and scholarship
- Innovative pieces that reimagine access, engagement, collaboration, and co-construction

We invite members of the Educational Theatre field to submit works that will share ideas, vocabularies, strategies, and techniques, centering on varying definitions and practices. That issue will publish in late 2024. Thereafter, look to the Verbatim Performance Lab for outreach and innovation from the NYU Steinhardt Program in Educational Theatre as well as the regional Leaders of Color Institute to be presented in collaboration with the American Alliance for Theatre and Education in 2024.

## SUGGESTED CITATION

Jones, J. P. (2024). Editorial: E pluribus unum. *ArtsPraxis, 11* (1), pp. i-xiv.

## REFERENCES

Bivens, J. (2024, April 2). Economic performance is stronger when Democrats hold the White House. *Economic Policy Institute.*

Bump, P. (2017, December 22). That coin toss election in Virginia? Dramatic. But it pales in comparison to other historic contests. *The Washington Post.*

Federal Trade Commission. (2024, March 21). FTC releases report on grocery supply chain disruptions.

Goldfarb, S., and DeBarros, A. (2024, April 14). 'Envy of the world'—U.S. economy expected to keep powering higher. *The Wall Street Journal.*

Jones, J. P. (2023). Editorial: Collective visioning. *ArtsPraxis, 10* (2), pp. i-xii.

Lewis, J. M., and Hensley, T. R. (1998). The May 4 shootings at Kent State University: The search for historical accuracy. Originally published by *The Ohio Council for the Social Studies Review, 34* (1), pp. 9-21.

Nehme, A. (2024, May 1). 'Fewer than half' of protesters arrested at Gould Plaza were students or faculty, Mills says. *Washington Square News.*

Oliphant, J. B., and Cerda, A. (2022, September 8). Republicans and Democrats have different top priorities for U.S. immigration policy. *Pew Research Center.*

Smithsonian Institute. (n.d.). E Pluribus Unum. from A gazetteer of the United States of America. Smithsonian Libraries and Archives.

Stern, M. J. (2024). *The Michelangelo Signorile Show.* [Radio broadcast]. Sirius XM.

*The Economist.* (2024, Mach 19). Five charts compare Democrats and Republicans on job creation.

US Department of State. (2018, March 19). The great seal.
YouGov. (2024). Most important issues facing the US.

## AUTHOR BIOGRAPHY

Jonathan P. Jones, PhD is a graduate from the Program in Educational Theatre at New York University, where he earned both an M.A. and a Ph.D. He conducted his doctoral field research in fall 2013 and in spring of 2014 he completed his dissertation, *Drama Integration: Training Teachers to Use Process Drama in English Language Arts, Social Studies, and World Languages.* He received an additional M.A. in English at National University and his B.A. in Liberal Arts from NYU's Gallatin School of Individualized Study. Jonathan is certified to teach English 6-12 in the state of California, where he taught Theatre and English for five years at North Hollywood High School and was honored with The Inspirational Educator Award by Universal Studios in 2006. Currently, Jonathan is an administrator, faculty member, coordinator of doctoral studies, and student-teaching supervisor at NYU Steinhardt. He serves on the editorial board for *Applied Theatre Research* and *Youth Theatre Journal,* and on the board of directors as well as chair of Research and Scholarship for the American Alliance for Theatre and Education (AATE) where he has recently been elected Chair-Elect and will serve as Chair from 2025-2027.

Jonathan has conducted drama workshops in and around New York City, London, and Los Angeles in schools and prisons. As a performer, he has appeared at Carnegie Hall, the Metropolitan Opera, Town Hall, The Green Space, St. Patrick's Cathedral, The Cathedral of St. John the Divine, The Southbank Centre in London UK, and the U.S. Capitol in Washington, D.C. Jonathan's directing credits include *Hamlet, Twelfth Night, Julius Caesar, Elsewhere in Elsinore, Dorothy Rides the Rainbow, A Midsummer Night's Dream, Bye Bye Birdie, The Laramie Project, Grease, Little Shop of Horrors*, and *West Side Story*. Assistant directing includes *Woyzeck* and *The Crucible*. As a performer, he has appeared at Carnegie Hall, the Metropolitan Opera, Town Hall, The Green Space, St. Patrick's Cathedral, The Cathedral of St. John the Divine, The Southbank Centre in London UK, Bord Gáis Energy Theatre in Dublin, and the U.S. Capitol in Washington, D.C. Production credits include co-producing a staged-reading of a new musical, *The Throwbacks*, at the New York Musical Theatre Festival and serving as assistant production manager and occasionally as stage director for the New York City Gay Men's Chorus, most recently directing *Quiet No More: A Celebration of Stonewall* at Carnegie Hall for World Pride, 2019.

At NYU, his courses have included Acting: Scene Study, American Musical Theatre: Background and Analysis, Assessment of Student Work in Drama, Development of Theatre and Drama I, Devising Educational Drama Programs and Curricula, Directing Youth Theatre, Drama across the Curriculum and Beyond, Drama in Education I, Drama in Education II, Dramatic Activities in the Secondary Drama Classroom, Methods of Conducting Creative Drama, Theory of Creative Drama, Seminar and Field Experience in Teaching Elementary Drama, Seminar and Field Experience in Teaching Secondary Drama, Shakespeare's Theatre, and World Drama. Early in his placement at NYU, Jonathan served as teaching assistant for American Musical Theatre: Background and Analysis, Seminar in Elementary Student Teaching, Theatre of Brecht and Beckett, and Theatre of Eugene O'Neill and worked as a course tutor and administrator for the study abroad program in London for three summers. He has supervised over 50 students in their student teaching placements in elementary and secondary schools in the New York City Area. Prior to becoming a teacher, Jonathan was an applicant services representative at NYU in the Graduate School of Arts and Science Enrollment Services Office for five years.

Recent publications include "And So We Write": Reflective Practice in Ethnotheatre and Devised Theatre Projects in *LEARNing Landscapes, 14* (2), Let Them Speak: Devised Theatre as a Culturally Responsive Methodology for Secondary Students in Routledge Companion to Theatre and Young People (edited by Selina Busby, Charlene Rajendran, and Kelly Freebody; forthcoming), Paradigms and Possibilities: A Festschrift in Honor of Philip Taylor (2019), and Education at Roundabout: It's about Turning Classrooms into Theatres and the Theatre into a Classroom (with Jennifer DiBella and Mitch Mattson) in Education and Theatres: Beyond the Four Walls (edited by Michael Finneran and Michael Anderson; 2019). His book Assessment in the Drama Classroom: A Culturally Responsive and Student-Centered Approach was published by Routledge in winter 2023/24.

Recent speaking engagements include Communing with the Ancestors—a keynote lecture for Amplify & Ignite: A Symposium on

Research and Scholarship (AATE/NYU, 2024) and featured guest spots on Fluency with Dr. Durell Cooper Podcast, speaking about Origins, Inspirations, and Aspirations, and Conversations in Social Justice Podcast, York St. John University, speaking about Activism and Race within University Teaching and Research (2021); panel moderation for AATE Leaders of Color Institute (We Will Not Be Erased: Combating Censorship and Book Bans in Theatre by, for, and about Youth, 2024 and Cultivating Spaces for LOC in Educational and 'Professional' Theatre Settings - Opening Keynote with Daphnie Sicre and José Casas, 2022), invited workshops for AATE Theatre in Our Schools (Reimagining Drama Curriculum: The Gradual Release of Responsibility Framework, Locating Order in the Chaos: Revisiting Assessment in the Drama Classroom and Stage to Page: Reimagining the Teacher/Practitioner Role in Scholarship) and the AATE National Conference (Classroom Justice: Culturally Responsive, Student-Centered Assessment in the Drama Classroom and Pandemic Positives: What Do We Keep? Looking Backwards to Move Forward); invited workshops for the 2024 NYC Arts in Education Roundtable (Assessment in the Drama Classroom: A Student-Centered Approach), LondonDrama, 2023 Dorothy Heathcote NOW conference in Aberdeen, Scotland (Assessment in the Drama Classroom; and co-facilitation with David Montgomery: *The Bear That Wasn't*: A Process Drama Investigating Identity and *The Last Book in the Universe*: A Process Drama Unpacking the Consequences of Book-Banning); an invited lecture on Performance as Activism at the Research-Based Theater Seminar, Washington, D.C. Citizen Diplomacy Fund Rapid Response COVID-19 Research-Based Theater Project, The COVID Monologues, part of the Citizen Diplomacy Action Fund for US Alumni Rapid Response made possible by the US Department of State and Partners of the Americas (2020); a keynote lecture on Drama and Education: Why and How for the Drama and Education Conference, Shanghai, China (2020); and an invited lecture, On Creativity, for the University of Anbar, Iraq (2020). Upcoming engagements include a workshop on Assessment in the Drama Classroom for the 2024 American Alliance for Theatre and Education Conference and as a roundtable discussion leader for the Educational Theatre Association's 2024 Conference.

In addition to his responsibilities at NYU, Jonathan teaches Fundamentals of Public Speaking, History of Theatre, and Introduction

Editorial: E Pluribus Unum

to Theatre at CUNY: Borough of Manhattan Community College.

# A Collective Vision for a Future in the Arts through Community and Civic Engagement Programs

**SHARON COUNTS**

PARSONS SCHOOL OF DESIGN, THE NEW SCHOOL

## ABSTRACT

*The arts have the power to effect change and animate democracy by demonstrating the public value of creative work that contributes to a larger social good. In this accelerated moment of radical change, the arts are being more consciously used as a way to engage communities around achieving civic goals and to create positive connections. A major tension in the field right now revolves around how to galvanize our collective resources and knowledge toward building a more sustainable future for theater at large. This article centers the use of civic and community engagement programs as one prominent and effective method that can foster synergy with communities that arts organizations and theaters engage and seek to engage. Many theaters are using community engagement programs to ignite community conversations and address past inequities. A case study highlights how one regional theater, Mid-Sized City Theater (MCT), a pseudonym, used community and civic engagement programs to promote reimagining their organization as a civic institution and to rebuild relationships with their community. The pursuit to improve relationships between theaters and communities using community engagement programs is one way this sector is working to address historical inequities for cultural workers, artists, and participants in the arts.*

The arts have the power to effect change and animate democracy by demonstrating the public value of creative work that contributes to a larger social good. In recent years, there has been increased focus on how "art can allow us to develop a new shared understanding of the world that. . . can move the barometer of social change towards equity and justice" (Desai, 2020). Traditionally, the arts have roots in social and civic justice, which have been used to accelerate and inspire learning around social justice issues (Murphy, 2002). However, the global pandemic and racial reckoning of 2020 deeply impacted the American theater in myriad ways, and had a direct correlation to an unraveling seen across the entire landscape (Paulson, 2024). A major tension in the field right now revolves around how to galvanize our collective resources and knowledge toward building a more sustainable future for theater at large. It is time for theater to employ new strategies to address systemic issues that we simply can't ignore or wash over with positive euphemisms. Theater at large needs to pivot away from a business model that was created in the mid-twentieth century in order to create solutions for its continued survival. In this accelerated moment of change, where consumers have prioritized participation in purpose-driven organizations, success in the arena of civic engagement is inextricably tied to the overall success of any arts organization (Benoit-Bryan & Jenetopolus, 2021).

Theater is facing an industry-wide epidemic of loss. Over the last 4 years, a large number of cultural organizations and theaters across the United States have closed their doors permanently, unable to sustain their business in this current climate (Paulson, 2024). The stakes are high, we are grappling with the continued existence of the American theater. I will center the use of civic and community engagement programs as one method that can positively impact the restoration of this sector and its relationships with the communities they serve and seek to serve. The notion of community itself is also evolving, "One of the challenges in this reinvention of community is the place within it of the arts and engagement with the arts, traditionally at the heart of many community rituals and celebrations" (Finneran & Anderson, 2019, p. 22).

Historically, in the arts sector there has been some confusion, resistance, and a lack of cohesion about the term community engagement. For the purpose of this article, I use a definition of community engagement from Americans for the Arts: "Activities undertaken by an arts organization as a part of a mission strategy designed to build deep relationships between the organization and the community in which it operates for the purpose of achieving mutual benefit" (Johnson, 2019).

Values-driven civic and community engagement work in the arts has risen in its stature and can no longer be considered secondary to the work of theaters and arts organizations. A connection has been drawn between the potential benefits of this work as it relates to the prospect of affecting community sustainability (Moldavanova & Wright, 2019). To strategically design the way forward, I believe that theater as a sector will need to use civic and community engagement work as one prominent and effective methodology that can foster synergy with communities they engage. The very nature of the relationship between arts organizations and communities continues to shift:

> It aspires to looking beyond the stages…and instead to interrogate how these theaters engage in a range of ways with their communities, framing the theaters not just as entertainment, but as leaders, framing the participants not just as audience but as members of a community of practice; and framing the practice not as alternative…but as core to the operation and policy of these theaters. (Finneran & Anderson, 2019, p. 24)

There are numerous benefits, both ethical and practical, for the pursuit of a civic- and community-focused arts agenda. Borwick (2012) asserted that arts organizations, for practical and ethical reasons, need to be more deeply connected to their communities; he contends they can accomplish this, demonstrating ways in which engagement can aid organizations. Many theaters are using community engagement, civic engagement, public programs, outreach and/or impact programs, to ignite community conversations, address past inequities and to repair and rebuild relationships with communities that have been historically excluded from a given theater, or theater itself.

I conducted a case study in which I analyzed how one regional theater, which I will refer to as Mid-Sized City Theater (MCT), a pseudonym, used community and civic engagement programs to promote reimagining their organization as a civic institution. Engagement programs are important components of programming developed and implemented by MCT while undergoing a significant shift in its mission. MCT was transitioning from being a predominantly producing and presenting organization to becoming a civic institution. As this study commenced, the new vision for MCT was to capture the collective imagination and build community through joy-filled theatrical activities that lead to a greater understanding of ourselves and each other. It was a notable and weighty shift for an arts organization to move toward becoming a civic institution that intended to use community engagement programming as a tool to support building community. Building community partnerships is fundamental to the success of engagement work, "Partnerships are one way through which we can combat some of the challenges of a liquid modernity, but also make theater programs beyond the main stage relevant and engaging for non-traditional audiences" (Finneran & Anderson, 2019, p. 26).

These varied terms (i.e., community engagement, civic engagement, public programs, outreach programs, impact programs) carry with them a variety of connotations, which were described as demeaning by several of the people I interviewed. Rhianna (a pseudonym), the strategic partnership consultant, addressed this when asked how she felt about the term "community engagement." She shared that she preferred to "talk about showing up for the community and having an impact. So, I'll use community impact ideas." She described MCT's community impact as "a level of engagement" and "a reciprocal term." She added, "I don't dislike it [community engagement]. I just think people overuse it."

Another staff member at MCT, Luisa (a pseudonym), the director of artistic partnerships and innovation, also took issue with the term community engagement and how it is used interchangeably with the term outreach:

> I tend to not use the word community engagement or even civic engagement. I'm not super interested in arguing about what words are right or wrong, but those words don't usually come out of my vocabulary when I'm talking about what I'm doing. And I would say it's maybe part of the way that the field talks about that work is why I tend to not position myself inside of it because often the field talks about community programs as, it's sometimes called outreach. . . I think they're not intended to be interchangeable. . . it's the White institutions reaching out to the Black and Brown audiences and trying to get them to do something. And that just does not feel like a relationship, ever. I don't want a theater to engage me as a Brown person myself. So, I tend to not use that phrasing.

Clearly, the ambiguity around how these terms are seen through the lens of racial equity has not been adequately addressed in the theater field or by the institutions using the terms. Borwick (2012) frames this debate:

> Most outreach that is undertaken is done "for" the community, assuming that the arts organizations understand what art the community needs. To be effective, successful engagement must be done "with" the community based on reciprocal, mutually beneficial relationships with the organizations or communities being served. Indeed, the very word "outreach" implies an unequal relationship: the "outreacher" is central and those "reached" are peripheral and in need of service. (p. 33)

Hager & Winlker (2012) assert that the arts sector seeks to promote civic engagement to advance connection and challenge assumptions. As a recent Culture Track report demonstrates, the cultural sector has an inclusion problem (Benoit-Bryan & Jenetopolus, 2021). Owing to the convergence of the pandemic and racial reckoning, arts organizations, no matter their size or geographic location "need to be in genuine dialogue with their audiences, participants, and communities as they decide how they can contribute and serve" (Benoit-Bryan & Jenetopolus, 2021). Paradoxically, the diversity in the principles and objectives driving this work, in addition to varying practices of implementing this work, have contributed to the wide-ranging definitions and intentions of this work in practice (Mutibwa, 2017). Clara (a pseudonym), the director of artistic producing, aligned with Luisa's earlier point in our second interview:

> Community engagement now sort of encompasses pretty much anything under the sun. It's a really useless term, I think. But importantly, it has become synonymous with Black and Brown people. It's synonymous with poor people and synonymous with the POC [people of color] leaders creating these initiatives.

The term community engagement itself has been racialized and endowed with negative connotations from the perspective of several staff members at MCT, due in part to how predominantly White institutions have used engagement as a tool to build relationships with communities of color. The lack of clarity in defining this work impacts our ability to advocate for it.

To build relationships with various communities, both in and outside of the arts sector (i.e., internal and external), MCT first needed to address what community means to them, which communities they are already engaging with, and the communities with which they wanted to build new relationships and partnerships. In an interview with Serena (a pseudonym), the artistic director, we discussed her perspective on whether MCT has a coherent understanding of the community it serves:

> What we see in other people's mission statements referring to "the community" . . . the plural, pluralizing communities [in the mission statement], was an attempt at making visible that we have many constituents and many communities that we should be engaging with. . . but, you know, it's more nuanced than that. And I think our job is to find the nuance. And so, my experience of MCT is that we're getting a better understanding that we have multiple constituencies, and that they sometimes have or often have divergent opinions and needs.

There has been a swell of sentiment that supports the notion that Americans no longer view arts and culture organizations as interdependent actors in systems that support their communities (Slover Linett, 2022). The ethos has shifted and there is now a demand to have our arts and culture organizations work with communities to create substantive public value (Slover Linett, 2022). More specifically, the public's desire for rootedness takes many forms, such as collaborative decision making and a desire to see more artwork that is a juxtaposition between professionally produced and community created productions. Rootedness and cohesion are vital in creating a common vision for a collective future in the arts. In the interview process, it became apparent that this is easier said than done, due in part to the misalignment of terms and practices that differentiate outreach and community engagement work. This points to a growing need for intersectional awareness and the eradication of silos. ""The siloing we have witnessed…of different disciplines and sectors has done little to prepare our education sector, theaters and our community for the looming challenges that will require citizens to be skilled collaborators" (Finneran & Anderson, 2019, p.27).

    A pursuit to improve conditions and connectivity between arts organizations and communities is one way that this sector is working to address equity, justice, and opportunity for cultural workers and participants in the arts. The multidimensional approach of engagement work in the arts has demonstrated capacity to respond to social justice issues and human suffering in a creative and connected way. Cultivating a broader sense of community and working together at MCT to enact the mission shift toward becoming a civic institution, became a unifying force that brought staff together around these efforts. However, there was an exodus of staff and board members who felt strongly that this shift was too far afield from the founding mission.

    One of the largest contributing factors that leads to building positive connections between an arts organization and the communities it serves, or aims to serve, is trust. Trust building is a reciprocal process that demands consistency over time. The discovery process for building consistent and trusting relationships with communities happens through meaningful connections and collaboration. It also happens through the building of equitable pipelines for staff, artists, board members, and community partnerships. Slover Linett (2022) frames trust-building as a three-step iterative cycle of 1) consistent action that 2) meets community needs and is 3) communicated as evidence. The world of theater and the arts are fascinating and productive laboratories for innovation and change.

For trust building to be impactful, a collective agreement around terms and practices must be reached through a reciprocal process between partners and communities.

The arts are a conduit for equity and are a place where we can be most inclusive. The conventional positioning of a theater or performing arts organization is to produce and present live performances. Paulo Freire, the Brazilian educator and activist, reminds us that the culture itself seeks to either maintain or transfigure social structures (Freire, 1992). Arts organizations do not necessarily make community or civic engagement integral to their mission. However, in ongoing cultural equity conversations, the notion of community and civic engagement programs as ancillary is rooted in limiting beliefs that belong to another era. The findings in this study demonstrate an arts and culture sector that is hungry for relatedness, meaning, and innovation, against the backdrop of a shifting landscape. Arts organizations must now be compelled to frame priorities around the possibility of creating a social transformation, toward just and equitable conditions in the arts. Many arts organizations have made this shift toward including civic and community engagement programs as essential components of their work and needed to remain relevant in the current cultural landscape.

The racial reckoning of 2020 served as a catalyst for deep reflection and fundamental change in the arts and culture sector as it pertains to equity and inclusion (Parker-Pope, 2021). Rahm Emanuel, former chief of staff for President Obama, famously issued what is now known as "Rahm's Rule" in the wake of the 2008 financial crisis, "You never want a serious crisis to go to waste" (Weidinger & Sprunt, 2022). The pandemic's pause allowed arts organizations to make progress on the longstanding challenges of inequities in this sector, finding positive opportunities in a time of crisis and not letting it go to waste. It is time for arts organizations to take actionable steps that go beyond the performative statements made in the wake of George Floyd, inclusive of shifting the value proposition of engagement work in this sector. This response will also require a repositioning of leadership and power structure dynamics.

The cultural paradigm of exclusionary practices in the arts and culture sector has a long and sustained history as old as the injustices of slavery and segregation (Walker-Khune, 2005). It is critical that arts organizations shift this narrative to "rebuild the structural economy and moral economy at the same time" (Joseph, 2024). Shifting the narrative will also allow innovation to continue around the use of theater and engagement work as a means to bring communities together. It will contribute to addressing the industry-wide challenge of ever-diminishing theater audiences. Reframing best practices through an antiracist lens is something that all arts organizations need to implement, inclusive of areas such as leadership, staffing, programming, and finances. Systemic racism, also labeled as institutional racism, is referred to as a "silent opportunity killer" and defined in the arts and social justice as "the blind interaction between institutions, policies, and practices that inevitably perpetuates barriers to opportunities and racial disparities. Conscious and unconscious racism continue to exist in our society" (Grantmakers, 2009).

Community and civic engagement programs have long been used to address social change. Borwick (2012) describes community engagement as a mission strategy to build deep relationships of trust and understanding, through which outreach can expand. There is an assertion here that arts organizations, for practical and ethical reasons, need to be more deeply connected to their communities. Borwick (2012) maintains that arts organizations can accomplish this by demonstrating ways in which engagement can aid organizations in achieving that goal: "There are numerous reasons, both moral and practical, for pursuit of a community focused arts agenda both for arts organizations and for communities" (p. 26). Values-driven civic and community engagement programs can no longer be considered secondary to the work of arts organizations. With a goal of creating dialogue with communities around various social issues, community engagement programs are being used by arts organizations to address the challenge of differentiating between relational and transactional processes (Grams & Farrell, 2008).

Leadership must also reevaluate budgets and fundraising strategies to support the development of new roles and programs with designated budget line items. Without financial support, mission statements that espouse a commitment to community and civic engagement are meaningless. Audiences and communities want alignment between their values and the organizations they support, as do the cultural workers who are the backbone of this sector (Slover Linett, 2022). This reframing will motivate arts organizations to invest in community engagement, staff, programs, and civic initiatives. Equitable resources will need to be allocated to actualize programs that fulfill their new mission statements. This new model for an equitable future, for any arts organization, places engagement at the center. How the arts community works to solve and address the fundamental needs of workers, artists and community members requires deep reflection, experimentation, and collaboration. However, these processes must happen concurrently for more holistic success in the arena of change management (Cameron, 2018).

For an organization to make civic and community engagement programs as relevant to their mission as the art that they create and produce, those changes will need to be supported by the board and leadership. It is critical that those changes be represented in an organization's strategic plans, with capital that demonstrates those core values. Arts based civic and community engagement programs provide demonstrated benefits in addressing issues of social justice, diversity, equity, and inclusion. Grantmakers for the Arts characterizes the lack of diversity in the arts and culture sector as "one of the most important issues for the cultural sector to address in the twenty-first century" (Cuyler, 2015). Cultural workers have a responsibility to audiences and communities to listen, to strive to understand, and to respond through creative innovations. The recommendations offered here focus on one aspect of the social impact of the arts—their influence on community and civic engagement. A desire for change, or for doing things differently, generally comes from a place of dissatisfaction or in response to some kind of pain (Schein, 2017).

Cultural workers and arts researchers will continue to seek ways to make meaning of how our society has been altered by the pandemic and racial reckoning of 2020, and how those seminal events have impacted the American Theater. Dias & Sayet (2018) discuss how theater may function as a space for needed healing industry-wide. Theater and the arts will continue to be vital as a place to exchange ideas and to confront the multiplicity of human experiences. Community and civic engagement programs will continue to be utilized to understand and represent the full range of the diversity of our lived experiences. The arts are and always will be a place for truthful expression. Communities will continue to congregate in shared spaces to create new experiences collaboratively and communally. Theater will always find a way to embrace curiosity and openness, and to encounter other visions of truth—and through that, a better understanding of who we are. When we trust the wisdom that lives and resides in those who are marginalized to tell their own stories on their own terms, theater can continue to evolve for our audiences and our communities. Theater will continue to operate as a catalyst for change that will help advance and progress our society, and I will continue to be hopeful for the reimagined future that we are building together.

## SUGGESTED CITATION

Counts, S. (2024). A collective vision for a future in the arts through community and civic engagement programs. *ArtsPraxis, 11* (1), pp. 1-13.

## REFERENCES

Benoit-Bryan, J., & Jenetopolus, M. (2021, July). Culture and community in a time of transformation. Culture Track.

Borwick, D. (2012, August 27). The eightfold path to community engagement. *Arts Journal*.

Cameron, B. (2018). Claiming value, illuminating common purpose. In E. Rosewell & R. Shane (Eds.), *Arts and cultural management: critical and primary sources (Vol. 1)*. Concord Theatricals.

Cuyler, A. C. (2020). Access, diversity, equity, and inclusion in cultural organizations. Routledge.

Desai, D. (2020). Educating for social change through art: A personal reckoning. *Studies in Art Education, 61* (1), pp. 10–23.

Dias, A., & Sayet, M. (2018, May 27). Decolonizing theatre/la descolonización del teatro. *HowlRound Theatre Commons*.

Desai, D. (2020). Educating for social change through art: A personal reckoning. *Studies in Art Education, 61* (1), pp. 10–23.

Finneran, M., & Anderson, M. (Eds.). (2019). *Education and theatres: Beyond the four walls*. Springer International Publishing.

Freire, P. (1992). *Pedagogy of hope: Reliving pedagogy of the oppressed*. Continuum.

Grams, D., & Farrell, B. (Eds.). (2008). *Entering cultural communities: Diversity and change in the nonprofit arts*. Rutgers University Press.

Grantmakers in the Arts. (2009). Structural racism.

Hager, M. A., & Winkler, M. K. (2012). Motivational and demographic factors for performing arts attendance across place and form. *Nonprofit and Voluntary Sector Quarterly, 41* (3), pp. 474-496.

Johnson, C. (2019, March 29). Audience engagement is not community engagement. Americans for the Arts.

Joseph, M. B. (2024, January 5). Marc Bamuthi Joseph on artists as leaders of collective healing. Ford Foundation.

Moldavanova, A. V., & Wright, N. S. (2019). How nonprofit arts organizations sustain communities: Examining the relationship between organizational strategy and engagement in community sustainability. *The American Review of Public Administration, 50* (3), pp. 244–259.

Murphy, P. (2002). *Civic Justice: From Greek antiquity to the modern world*. Humanity Books.

Mutibwa, D. H. (2017). 'Sell[ing] what hasn't got a name': An exploration of the different understandings and definitions of 'community engagement' work in the performing arts. *European Journal of Cultural Studies, 22* (3), pp. 345–361.

Parker-Pope, T. (2021, January 9). Recycle your pandemic habits. *The New York Times*.

Paulson, M. (2023, July 23). A crisis in America's theaters leaves prestigious stages dark. *The New York Times*.

Schein, E. H. (2017). *Organizational culture and leadership*. Wiley.

Slover Linett. (2022). *Rethinking relevance, rebuilding engagement: Findings from the second wave of a national survey about culture, creativity, community and the arts*. Slover Linett.

Walker-Kuhne, D. (2005). *Invitation to the party building bridges to the arts, culture, and community*. Theatre Communications Group.

Weidinger, M., & Sprunt, T. (2022, September 9). The "never let a serious crisis go to waste" crowd strikes again. *The American Enterprise Institute*.

**AUTHOR BIOGRAPHY**

Sharon Counts is an Assistant Professor of Business and Design Strategies at Parsons School of Design, The New School. Her research-led creative practice explores the efficacy of social impact and community engagement programs in the arts. Sharon has worked broadly as an artistic producer, director, and designer of artistic experiences and programs that prioritize equitable access to culture. She works at the intersection of the arts and innovation, applying strategic design principles to the development of artistic programming. Sharon holds an Ed.D. in Leadership and Innovation from NYU, an MA in Educational Theatre from NYU, and a BFA in Acting from Emerson College.

# "We Can Help!": Using Creative Drama to Explore Social Justice in Youth Theatre

## MADDIE N. ZDEBLICK

COLLEGE OF EDUCATION, UNIVERSITY OF WASHINGTON, SEATTLE

## NOËLLE GM GIBBS

SAN JOSÉ STATE UNIVERSITY

## ABSTRACT

*Theatre can be a powerful tool for exploring social justice issues, but it can also reproduce whiteness, ableism, and other systemic oppressions. As theatre educators—constrained by many competing demands on our time, resources, and energy—we want to know: how can we leverage our teaching artistry to authentically explore social justice issues with the young people and adults in our communities? Speaking from our experiences at a nonprofit theatre in a majority-white, upper-middle-class community, we offer creative drama as a model for integrating this kind of social justice education into youth musical theatre production camps. We explore the tools that creative drama offers for supporting youth and teaching artists in exploring issues related to inclusion, diversity, equity, and accessibility; understanding our relationships with oppressive systems; and taking action to transform them. Then, we demonstrate how this can look in practice. We outline a process through which we developed two creative drama adventures and share stories of how these dramas unfolded. Finally, we surface some lingering tensions about our and our students' identities and how they inform our ongoing work. In sharing these stories and tensions, we invite you to consider how creative drama might support you and your communities.*

Fifty kindergarten-through-eighth-grade students gathered after lunch on the first day of our flagship musical theatre production summer camp. It was time to get down to work on *The SpongeBob Musical: Youth Edition*. Suddenly, Dr. Inkling, an octopus bearing a striking resemblance to our theatre's administrative assistant, burst into the room covered in blue tape, desperate for assistance.

"Help! Help! Someone threw all this blue tape in my ocean and now it's stuck all over me!" Dr. Inkling cried. The kindergartners looked shocked. The eighth graders giggled. Everyone's eyes were glued to Dr. Inkling, or "Inky" for short.

Earlier that morning, the camp had played a game of "The Wind Blows" as an icebreaker activity. Each actor had been given a piece of blue tape to mark a spot on the ground, and at the end of the game, they had peeled up their tape and made a giant ball, which supposedly made its way to the trash. However, when Dr. Inkling appeared, we learned that the scraps of tape had found their way to the ocean! Soon, we were hooked on this octopus' drama and eager to help her solve the problem of her increasingly polluted ocean—which was getting worse! The Ocean Council, in charge of all major decisions, wanted to build a giant hotel development right where Dr. Inky lived. This was sure to make the pollution worse, but the Ocean Council did not want to listen to Dr. Inky's appeals. "We can help!" offered a student.

Summer camp staff acted surprised to see Inky, but of course, they were expecting her. It was all part of the plan. But how did Dr. Inkling—or the idea of her—make it to our intimate summer camp stage in the first place (see Figure 1)? And how could this fictional octopus covered in tape help us explore social justice with our students?

**Figure 5:** Maddie (left) facilitates a conversation between Dr. Inky (right) and PVTC summer campers about the wasteful nature of theatre.

For many theater artists, the link between theatre and justice is self-evident, expressed easily through cliché—theatre changes hearts and minds, celebrates diversity, and invites everyone to speak their truth. While there is truth in these truisms—theatre and the arts can uplift counter-narratives (Gallagher et al., 2017), prompt critical reflexivity (Tanner, 2018), and provoke empathy (Eisner, 1998; Troxler et al., 2023)—there is also an underlying tension. Despite repeated calls for change, the culture of theatre and theatre education in the United States remains steeped in ableism and white supremacy (*We See You W.A.T.*, 2020; Zdeblick, 2023a). Constrained by ever-intensifying and competing demands on our time, energy, and resources, theatre educators want to know: What can we do, in our settings, to shift this culture toward justice for all communities? How can we bring young people along with us on our journey? And how can the tools we already have as theatre artists support us in this work?

In this paper, we will explore how, through creative drama, a form of scaffolded dramatic play (Ward, 1960), our nonprofit theatre has connected our summer camp shows to issues of inclusion, equity, diversity, and accessibility (IDEA). We have supported our kindergarten through eighth-grade students (and our staff) in developing age-appropriate understandings of systems of oppression, investigating our relationships with these systems, and taking action to reshape our community and the wider world. And, we have done so alongside fast-paced rehearsal schedules that culminate in traditionally polished and lively junior musicals. Integrating socially-engaged creative drama into our curriculum has broadened and deepened our work; yes, young artists leave our camps knowing more about theatre, but, perhaps more importantly, they also leave seeing themselves as change agents. We offer our work not as a one-size-fits-all model, but as an example of how authentic social justice engagement might be integrated into more mainstream theatre education curricula. While this work can go deep—it usually goes deeper than we expect—all you need to get started is one or two enthusiastic educators, a little bit of time, whatever spare props and costumes you have lying around, and a willingness to say "yes, and…"!

In the following sections, we will introduce ourselves and our context before diving into some of the theory that animates our creative drama work. Next, we will outline the steps of our process: selecting a theme, facilitating staff learning, bringing in outside materials, creating a story with a problem, interspersing episodes of the story throughout a rehearsal process, and embracing the inevitable follow-up conversations that arise with students. We will bring these steps to life by sharing stories from two creative dramas that we facilitated alongside more traditional musical theatre productions: *The Drama of Sprinkles the Unicorn (2022)* alongside *Frozen Jr.* and *The Drama of Dr. Inkling the Octopus (2023)* alongside *The SpongeBob Musical: Youth Edition.* Then, we will surface some of the ongoing tensions that we, two white nondisabled cis-female educators in a privileged community, continue to hold as we engage in this work. Finally, we will discuss what this model might offer other theatres and theatre artists struggling to do it all—produce fun, vibrant, full-scale musicals and engage students in meaningful social justice learning.

## INTRODUCING OURSELVES AND OUR CONTEXT

Before we go further, we (Maddie and Noëlle), would like to introduce ourselves. Though we worked together to develop and facilitate the creative drama adventures described in this article and share many salient identities, we have distinct professional roles and perspectives. We recognize that our identities influence the experiences we've had in theatre education and that our perspective is just one perspective. We are both deeply committed to social justice in theatre and theatre education. The work we're sharing with you played out at Portola Valley Theatre Conservatory (PVTC), a nonprofit theatre whose mission is to create community and inspire individuals to discover their unique passion through pursuit of excellence in theatre arts. Most of PVTC's students and staff live within a 30-minute radius of Portola Valley, a majority-white, highly-educated suburb of San Francisco, CA, with a median household income nearly double that of the surrounding metropolitan area.

I (Maddie) grew up fifteen minutes away from PVTC. I am a cis-gender, straight, white, non-disabled woman, scholar, and teacher with ten years of experience teaching theatre to disabled and nondisabled youth and adults. My brother—who adores theatre—is labeled with intellectual and developmental disabilities. As a result, I've spent much of my academic and professional life focused on making inaccessible theatre spaces more accessible. My whiteness and socioeconomic privilege mean that I've experienced fewer barriers in this work than someone holding different identities. I directed PVTC's production of *Frozen Jr.* in the summer of 2022 and returned to campus as a scholar in residence in 2023 who, among other responsibilities, facilitated PVTC's IDEA initiatives for *The SpongeBob Musical: Youth Edition*.

I (Noëlle) have been in leadership at PVTC for fifteen years and am currently the Executive Director. I produced the production of *Frozen Jr.* that Maddie directed and, in the summer of 2023, I directed *SpongeBob: The Musical Youth Edition.* Like Maddie, I am a straight, white, cis-gender, non-disabled woman who grew up near PVTC. I have always had my basic needs met and have had abundant access to arts and education. Through my years at PVTC, I have witnessed first-hand the transformative power of theatre by aiming to create a space where our world expands through the act of storytelling and empathy-building.

From its inception, PVTC has been committed to inclusive practices, looking for ways to involve all members of the community in the process of making excellent and transformative theatre. While we have anecdotal history to illustrate how this value plays out in practice, like other theatres, we wanted to do more in the wake of 2020's racial justice uprisings. Motivated by the national call for accountability in theatrical IDEA practices (*We See You W.A.T.*, 2020) and our desire to do more from our privileged space, PVTC grew serious about how values of inclusion flowed intentionally through our curriculum. Summer camp seemed like a great place to start. For one, students are with us for an extended period, usually six to seven hours per day. Unlike the school year, when we see students only once per week for an hour or two, summer camp affords us the time to integrate co-curricular activities into our programming that support the development of a performance-based activity.

## THEATER EDUCATION AND SOCIAL JUSTICE

We pause here to acknowledge the historically fraught relationship between theater education and social justice learning. As previously alluded to, scholars and activists have revealed the *injustice* of many traditional actor training practices. Through reinforcing normative ideas about which texts count as "canon" (Dyches, 2017), which stories and acting methods are "universal" (Dunn et al., 2020), which casting decisions are "colorblind" and "objective" (Schroeder-Arce, 2017), which bodies and minds appear "neutral" (Sandahl, 2005), and which voices sound "natural" and "free" (McAllister-Viel, 2021; Cahill & Hamel, 2022), theater educators often reproduce whiteness and ableism in our contexts (Zdeblick, 2023a). Despite what many theater educators might say about our work's inherent inclusivity (Brown, 2020), the link between theater and social justice is far from inevitable (Finneran & Freebody, 2015).

However, research has revealed how, through making deliberate pedagogical choices and engaging in ongoing self-reflection, theater educators can further social justice goals. Syler and Chen (2017) explored how, through considering students' identities in casting decisions, theater educators might support students' positive racial identity development. Horn (2017) described an applied theater project in which Black boys developed and facilitated an interactive workshop with local police officers that explored the racial dynamics of policing. Winn (2012) explored how a playwrighting program supported formerly incarcerated Black and Brown girls in navigating their relationships with systematic injustices. And Tanner (2018) described how his predominantly white students analyzed and illustrated how whiteness circulated within their own high school theater program. These examples illustrate how—with a particular focus on racial justice—theater educators have pursued social justice in their work. Scholars have also explored adapting theater education for special and inclusive education contexts, though much of this work has asked how theater educators might help solve the *problem* of *disability* (see e.g., Bailey 2010; 2021). In better alignment with disability justice activism (Sins Invalid, 2019), a smaller but growing body of research has instead asked how theater educators might help solve the *problem* of *ableism* (see e.g., Whitfield, 2022; Zdeblick, 2023b).

Against this tension-riddled—yet promising—theoretical backdrop, we found ourselves wondering how to meaningfully engage our young artists in social justice learning. In early 2022, I (Noëlle) was sitting at a board meeting talking about how we might integrate IDEA into our summer camp curriculum. To complicate things, our camp schedule was already jam-packed. There was inherent tension in wanting to expand our curriculum with justice, fully leaning into the joy, fun, and discovery of that process, while also teaching vocal harmonies, sewing costumes, rehearsing choreography, mastering transitions, training high school tech interns, and having fun with water balloons and popsicles. In our work with fifty students ranging in age from kindergarten through eighth grade, we hoped to provoke more than simple awareness. Our summer camp is located on the ancestral lands of the Ohlone people. Like us, our teaching staff and students are overwhelmingly white, upper or middle-class, highly educated, and non-disabled. We wanted our students to reflect on their relationships with difficult social issues, recognize their potential complicity, and imagine changes they might make individually and together to make the world a better, more just place. In other words, we hoped to engage our young actors in critical consciousness-raising. Critical consciousness (Freire, 1970), or understanding the social systems shaping our world and our role in transforming them, cannot be learned through passive listening. Instead, learners develop critical consciousness through practicing agency, transforming what they're given into something new (Sannino et al., 2016).

The connection between theatre education and critical consciousness-raising is well-established, particularly through Augusto

Boal's Theatre of the Oppressed (1979). For example, in Forum Theatre, a form of Theatre of the Oppressed, a team of actors presents an audience (called "spect-actors" to emphasize their agency) with a problem grounded in the real-life circumstances of their community. When the problem is well-developed, the actors pause, inviting the spect-actors to imagine how they might intervene to transform the given situation. Spect-actors take turns trying out their ideas onstage, building individual and collective capacity to transform their world. Theatre of the Oppressed methods have been used to develop critical consciousness among middle and high school students (Bhukhanwala, 2014; see e.g., Marín, 2007; Snyder-Young, 2011), teacher candidates (see e.g., Bhukhanwala et al., 2017; Souto-Manning et al., 2008), and teacher educators (see e.g., Stillman et al., 2019). However, we found far less evidence for using Theatre of the Oppressed techniques with students the age of our campers, some of whom were just five years old.

    We were talking about curriculum one day when we had a lightbulb moment: every summer, our staff had a tradition of putting on a weekly staff skit. We usually came up with a narrative framework that paralleled the story we were exploring onstage and then dipped into a mostly improvised "episode" of this skit weekly. The skit originated as an opportunity for staff performers to model onstage behavior to budding actors: cheating out, making physical choices, projecting loudly, enunciating, making eye contact—all the skills we were working on with young actors in rehearsal. I (Maddie) wondered, "Could the staff skit be doing more?" Based on my past work, particularly with Seattle Children's Theatre, we turned to creative drama. In creative drama, a form of improvisational role-play (Freeman et al., 2003), teachers and students play characters and collaborate to tell stories (Hallgren & Österlind, 2019). Critically, teachers endow students with "the mantle of the expert," meaning they position students in roles with more expertise than those played by the teacher (Heathcote & Herbert, 1985). Teachers guide students back and forth from in-character problem-solving to out-of-character reflection, and students' agency moves the plot forward. Since the 1960s, educators have recognized creative drama's potential to support students' critical consciousness development around social justice issues (García-Mateus, 2021). In the words of Streeter (2017), creative drama can provide "a platform to explore social issues and interrogate histories through embodied story-making, for both the facilitator and participant" (p. 88). By marrying theatrical modeling with creative drama, the staff skit morphed into a model for authentically integrating IDEA issues into our summer camp programming.

**THE MODEL**

In the two summers that followed, we developed the following working model. In this section, we will describe the process of developing two creative drama adventures over two consecutive summers, *The Drama of Sprinkles the Unicorn (2022)* and *The Drama of Dr. Inkling the Octopus (2023).* Following Adelman and others (2020), we invite you to consider how our identities as facilitators—and the identities of our students—impacted the choices we made. As you read, we invite you to learn from our experiences, taking up any practices that feel useful for your contexts and leaving behind those that don't.

*Selecting a Theme*

We always start our work by looking for themes that are authentic to the plays we're rehearsing. For example, when I (Maddie) directed *Frozen Jr.*, I thought about the character of Elsa and what she represents. Elsa was born physically and cognitively different—with magical powers—and raised to fear her differences. For this reason, disabled viewers have hailed her as Disney's "first disabled princess" (Resene, 2017). Inspired by Elsa, and informed by my background as a sister to a disabled brother and my research at the intersection of theatre, disability, and education (Zdeblick, 2023b, 2023a), I chose to explore Disability Justice (Sins Invalid, 2019) with my actors.

The following summer, when I (Noëlle) began working on *The SpongeBob Musical,* two possible IDEA-themed lenses struck me. On the one hand, I was interested in the xenophobia that Sandy Squirrel encounters as a land mammal among sea creatures. With mounting bias against immigration and general divisiveness within the US, validating a character who had been "othered" felt like a theme we could sink our teeth into. On the other hand, I was drawn to this idea of environmental justice and of how theatre-making as a practice is or is not sustainable. I began to wonder if we could produce an entire summer made from old set pieces, found objects, thrifted clothing, and recycled materials. The theme would embrace not just conversations about the ocean home of the characters living with Bikini Bottom, but also push PVTC towards more sustainable design and build practices. Another struggle that we—like so many other small theatres—face is a lack of storage space, so we find ourselves throwing away materials at the end of a production. What if we ended with less waste? Could we avoid ordering the dumpster at the end of camp? I floated the sustainability idea at our next production meeting and asked Maddie if sustainability could even fall within the IDEA umbrella. Maddie gave an enthusiastic "yes" and began talking about how environmental harms disproportionately impact the same populations who often experience racism and other forms of systemic injustice.

### *Facilitating Staff Learning*

Once our themes are selected for each summer, we immerse our entire summer camp staff in learning. For *Frozen Jr.,* this looked like engaging the whole staff in conversations about how ableism, the system that ascribes value to bodies and minds based on their proximity to constructs like "normal" (Lewis, 2022), showed up on our campus. It also looked like exploring Carolyn Lazard's *Accessibility in the Arts: A Promise and a Practice* (2019), a guide to creating more accessible art spaces. Since 2015, PVTC has always done a sensory-friendly "Access Preview" of all of our summer camp musicals, so disability was already on our minds. However, we knew we could go further, especially in terms of thinking about how ableism (and racism) showed up in our teaching when we praised certain ways of being and discouraged others.

For *The SpongeBob Musical: Youth Edition,* staff researched ways in which they could embrace sustainability in their designs and lessons. Our props designer mined our craft storage areas for supplies and drew from those for every project rather than purchasing new ones. She built Sandy's "Erruptor Interrupter" jetpack out of a cardboard box with empty paper towel rolls standing in for the propulsion jets, and bits of scrap ribbon as shoulder straps. She decorated it with paper scraps and paint. The prop looked awesome and did not waste any new materials. Our costume designer similarly explored existing costume stock and built pieces out of scrap fabric and existing pieces where she could. Our set designer collected bottle caps and used them to adorn a ship's steering wheel that was mounted to the front of the set. Staff had significant buy-in, even before the campers arrived!

**Finding Outside Resources**

The second step is to search for additional story materials to help even our youngest campers connect our production to our chosen IDEA theme. For *Frozen Jr.,* we selected the picture book, *Not Quite Narwhal* (Sima, 2017). In this story, a young unicorn, raised by narwhals, grows up feeling isolated by his differences. When he stumbles across a family of unicorns, he discovers his identity. However, rather than stay with the unicorns, he returns home, determined to find a way to live his truth surrounded by the narwhals he loves. I (Maddie) saw this narwhal's journey as a disability narrative, parallel to Elsa's. I hoped even our five-year-old campers would understand how this narwhal felt out of place, not through a fault of his own, but through a genuine mismatch between his body and his environment.

For *SpongeBob,* the perfect book, *Fur and Feather Stand Together* (Griswold, 2020), fell into our lap. The story spoke to the *SpongeBob* team immediately, as it is told from the perspective of "two unlikely friends—a puffin and a polar bear—joining together with their community to save the ice that is melting around them." The authors provide resources for teachers in classrooms to use the material and speak about why they as white people centered an indigenous young woman as their main human character. The book, both in theme and the ways it advocates beyond itself, aligned perfectly with the IDEA values we wanted to explore alongside *SpongeBob.*

**Creating a Parallel Problem**

Once we have selected a theme and engaged our staff in learning, we next create what we call "a parallel problem," a term I (Maddie) borrowed from Seattle Children's Theatre's Story Drama curriculum. Our goal is to create a problem that is related to, yet distinct from, the problems in the various source materials we're using, so that we can engage students in using their expert knowledge of our source materials to help a character solve it. For example, both Elsa in *Frozen Jr.* and the unicorn in *Not Quite Narwhal* experience feeling out of place in their communities. Inspired by this, we developed the character of Sprinkles, a unicorn (played by our delightfully expressive assistant choreographer, see Figure 2) who was unable to attend school with his fellow sea creatures because his body wasn't made to swim.

**Figure 6:** Sprinkles the Unicorn (horn "hidden" underneath a rainbow top hat) arrives at PVTC.

To explore sustainability alongside *SpongeBob* and the characters from *Fur and Feather Stand Together,* we turned to Dr. Inkling, the Octopus from our opening scene whose ocean had been invaded by blue tape. We learned from Dr. Inkling that she had spent her whole life researching ocean health, but was ignored by the Ocean Council, the rulers of the sea. Not only had our students' wasteful ways disturbed her in her retirement, but the Ocean Council was about to approve plans for a new, massive, wasteful underwater hotel. She desperately needed our students' help. Like SpongeBob, Dr. Inkling didn't feel strong enough to overcome this challenge on her own.

### *Activating the Story*

The next step in our process is to bring our story to life and engage students in solving the parallel problem. To launch each adventure, one or more teaching artists perform a 30-45 minute initial scene, with lots of audience engagement, to get our students excited. Usually, at least one other teaching artist participates out-of-character, mediating discussion between the characters onstage and the students. The scene doesn't have to be polished—we often write a short script that teaching artists have in hand and use as a jumping-off point for improvisation. When the scene ends, students are left with both an understanding of the problem and a hint of their role in it. Through three or four additional episodes, teaching artists and students work together to bring the problem to a climax and navigate its resolution. In these intermediate scenes, students try to solve the problem. As teaching artists, we say "yes, and…" to their agency and activate the consequences! Importantly, all of their attempts work (remember that they are the "experts"), but not completely. They leave some part of the problem unsolved; to resolve it completely, students must invite the main character of our creative drama to their show. Sometimes, we add co-curricular ways for students to engage with the problem in smaller groups with similar-aged peers. Finally, once students have performed, they meet with the main character one last time to arrive at a resolution. To explore what this looks like in practice, let's dive into *The Drama of Sprinkles the Unicorn* and *The Drama of Dr. Inkling the Octopus*!

*The Drama of Sprinkles the Unicorn.*

Remember Sprinkles, the unicorn growing up amongst sea creatures, distraught because he couldn't attend underwater school with his friends? Sprinkles came to PVTC looking for help, but when the students revealed they were producing a play, he panicked, thinking a theatre wouldn't be accessible for him either! Our students, who immediately recognized their own role in creating a space that didn't work for Sprinkles, were hooked. Though Sprinkles left this first episode in tears, he soon returned. Students suggested that he try wearing a costume—maybe if he looked more like a sea creature, he'd feel more at home with his peers. In walked another teaching artist, our costume designer! Speaking in a voice oddly reminiscent of Edna Mode, from *The Incredibles*, she informed Sprinkles in no uncertain terms that his tail would have to go. Our students rushed to Sprinkles' defense. In the words of one early elementary schooler, Sprinkles should "keep all of his body parts." He shouldn't have to change himself to belong. Instead, the world should change to welcome all of Sprinkles' intersecting identities.

The next time Sprinkles returned, I (Maddie) produced the book, *Not Quite Narwhal*, as a resource that might help us solve our problem. Sprinkles and our students listened with rapt attention as I read. When the story ended, Sprinkles was inspired, but he felt he needed one more story about community transformation and to get up the courage to return home. Our students suggested he attend a performance of *Frozen Jr.*, but again, the issue of accessibility arose. Unicorns don't often sit still in seats and quietly watch theatre. And they're often afraid of the dark. The students immediately thought of inviting Sprinkles to our Access Preview. Around this time, our youngest students began to beg for more time with Sprinkles. They were exhausted from rehearsals, and as it turned out, a social justice storytime with Sprinkles was just the thing to rejuvenate them for performances. After Sprinkles saw our show—which he loved—he felt brave enough to go back to the ocean and demand his friends welcome him as his full and complete self (See Figure 3).

Using Creative Drama to Explore Social Justice in Youth Theatre

**Figure 7:** Inspired by the students, Sprinkles returns to the ocean to see his narwhal friends.

In our last scene, Sprinkles returned to the ocean, only to find his friends trapped in a thick sheet of ice. The students suggested that maybe the very thing that made Sprinkles different (his unicorn horn) and his love for his community could thaw the ice. Referencing *Frozen Jr.*, a student called out, "Love will thaw!" It worked! And, more importantly, Sprinkles and his community learned to appreciate that the differences in their bodies and minds made them stronger. They could find a way to move together.

*The Drama of Dr. Inkling the Octopus.*

A year later, Dr. Inky stumbled into our theatre, covered in blue tape, distraught over our campers' wastefulness and her superiors' indifference to ocean health. When Dr. Inky learned that students were rehearsing a play, her anger intensified. Theatre was so wasteful! For the health of the planet, theatre should be abolished. Our students resisted—there had to be a way to keep doing theatre, but more sustainably. Dr. Inkling reluctantly agreed to stay her judgment, but only if the students worked together to imagine more sustainable ways of making theatre. She said she'd be back next week to check in on their progress. Now our students had a problem to solve: How could the choices they made in the next four weeks of camp impact Dr. Inkling's life for the better and rehabilitate theatre? In small groups, the students set to work.

First up, the campers went on a sustainability scavenger hunt across the PVTC campus. They noticed details that were environmentally friendly (e.g., recycling bins everywhere, a water fountain where reusable water bottles could be refilled) and places that needed work (e.g., a lack of compost, aerosol cans for spray painting). Subsequent small-group conversations varied based on the ages of campers involved. For example, our youngest students researched the rules about what could and could not be recycled, while our middle schoolers discussed the reasons for the issues they observed on campus (e.g., convenience, lack of services), their impacts on climate and ocean health, and the lower-income communities of color disproportionately affected by these impacts. In the second episode of our creative drama, impassioned campers reported their findings to me (Noëlle) and other members of the leadership team, demanding change. To motivate the next stage of our drama, the leadership team admitted students' observations were excellent, but their demands were overwhelming! We were too busy supporting their show to take on anything extra. To gather ideas on how to build a movement in the face of resistance, students turned to *Fur and Feather Stand Together*. Inspired by the story, a group of middle schoolers wrote a rap about the importance of using sustainable materials in our design practices. Elementary schoolers wondered about transitioning more of our lighting instruments to LEDs and suggested we raise money to replace our traditional fixtures. The camp co-authored a letter to our local waste management facility requesting that they consider offering composting service in our area (see Figure 4). All campers made posters celebrating sustainable practices.

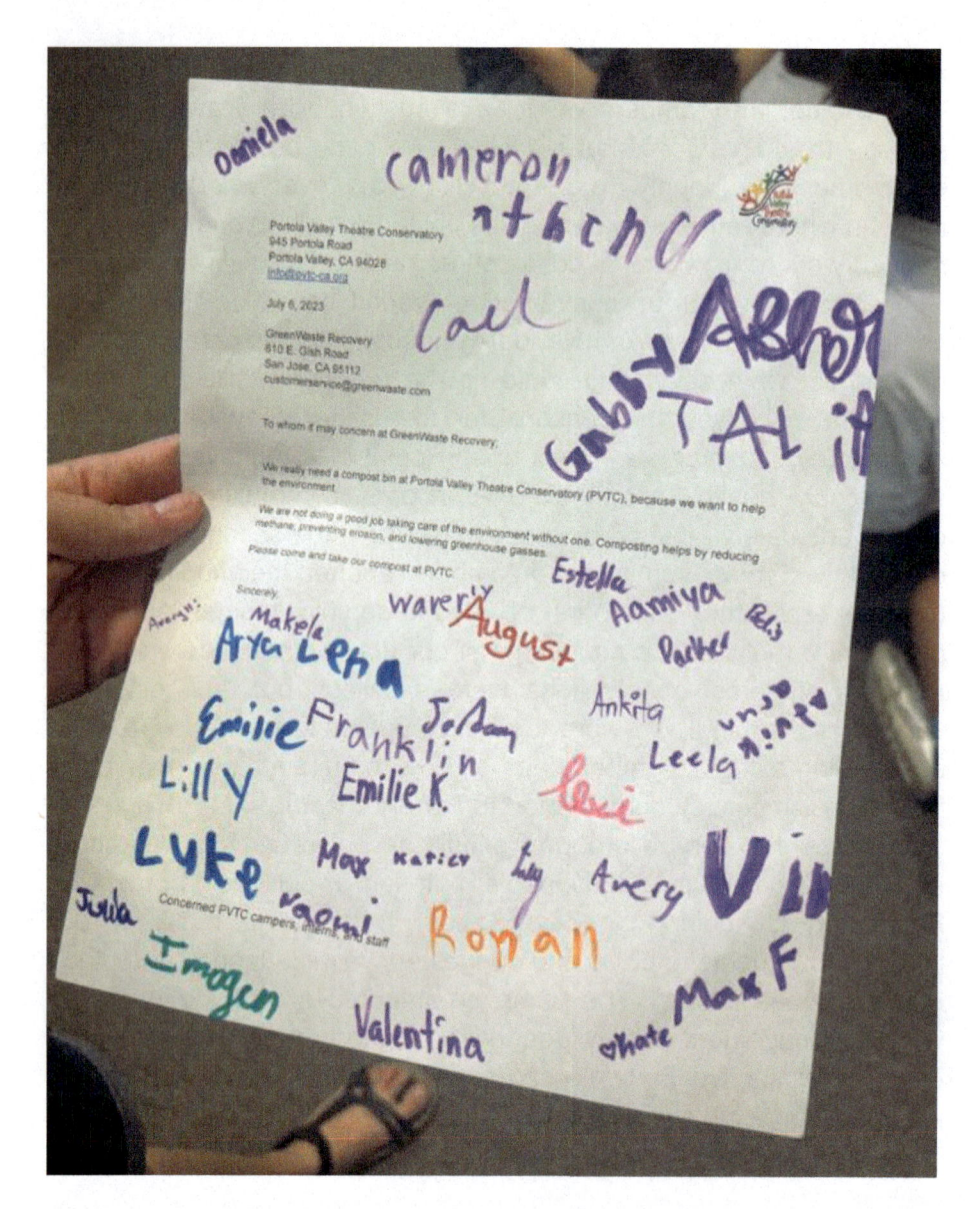

**Figure 8:** Students' letter to the local waste management agency, requesting compost pickup for our campus.

Students presented their work to the leadership team, which "convinced" us of sustainability's importance. Together, we started making small changes around campus. Inky was thrilled to hear about this progress when she returned to PVTC. She was so inspired that she built up the courage to go back to the Ocean Council to advocate against the hotel development in her ocean (see Figure 5). But the council did not budge! They believed their project signified progress, the way of the future! That is, of course, until the campers invited the Ocean Council to come see *SpongeBob*. Sitting in the audience of *SpongeBob,* the Ocean Council learned how even the littlest creature can make a big difference. After the show, the Ocean Council announced that they would be ending their ocean development project, to the joy of Dr. Inky! Through sharing their stories, onstage and off, students helped Dr. Inky change hers— and made our campus more sustainable along the way.

**Figure 9:** Dr. Inky advocates her case to the Ocean Council.

## *Following Up*

Inevitably, when we explore challenging issues with young people, they bring up challenging questions. These questions might surprise us, make us uncomfortable, or even force us to confront our own practices and complicity in systemic injustices. When these questions arise, it can be tempting to brush them aside with the excuse that we don't have time to explore them fully. As educators, it is our responsibility to be brave and make that time. Maybe it's after our show has opened, maybe it's in small group conversations with students who aren't in a particular rehearsal, but these questions deserve our full attention. If we let them, students' questions can transform the heart and soul of our work in profound and meaningful ways.

For example, when I (Maddie) was directing *Frozen Jr.*, a middle schooler interrupted rehearsal one day with some tough questions about mental health and accountability. From our creative drama, she knew that Elsa hadn't intended to freeze Arendell—she acted out of anxiety and shame about her physical and cognitive differences—but ultimately, Elsa had still caused harm. Why were we ok with crowning her queen? I panicked. I had forty kindergarten through eighth-grade students onstage learning the blocking for our show's finale. However, rather than shut this student down, I took a breath, emphasized what a good question she had, and promised to return to it soon. After their show had opened, I gathered all but the kindergarten students together onstage. We sat in a circle and discussed her question. Ultimately, we agreed she was right. While Elsa hadn't intended to cause harm, she had. And, by the end of the story, she was likely still dealing with trauma. I wondered aloud, "What might be a better resolution for Elsa than becoming Queen?" An eighth grader responded tentatively, "Therapy?" The rest of the circle cheered, "Therapy!"

In *The Drama of Dr. Inkling the Octopus*, students asked hard questions that demanded an immediate response. Recall how students worked in groups to conduct a sustainability scavenger hunt across the PVTC campus. On their journey around campus, a group of our students observed our set designer cutting styrofoam in the parking lot. As he chiseled out large cartoon flowers to attach to our set, tiny bits of white foam floated everywhere. The students were horrified. Maybe Dr. Inkling was right. Theatre was terrible for the planet! As a staff, we were embarrassed and ashamed. Students had caught us failing at exactly the thing we were trying to do. After camp, a core group of our staff came together to respond. We determined that our set designer had likely thought he was using a sustainable form of styrofoam, based on the product's advertising. We devised a plan to clean up the styrofoam and created a new policy explicitly banning styrofoam from new design projects. However, as the flowers had already been cut, we determined that the most sustainable thing we could do was use them. We apologized to our students and explained our plan for moving forward. Ultimately, we all learned a valuable lesson about moving towards justice: mistakes happen. It is our job to own them, learn from them, and find a way to move forward.

## TENSIONS AND CHALLENGES

Even as we've learned so much from these creative drama adventures, questions remain. For one, we continue to wonder about our role as facilitators of these dramas. We know how important it is to center marginalized voices in social justice learning; as straight, white, nondisabled women, should we be the ones leading these dramatic explorations? While we don't have an answer to this question, here are some of our ongoing thoughts. First, we welcome all of our summer camp teaching artists to help develop these dramas, but few hold marginalized identities (a symptom of systemic inequality in our organization and theatre more broadly). While we're actively working to diversify, we don't want to tokenize our current teaching artists of color by assuming they want to lead our community in this work. We're cautious about using our positionalities as excuses for avoiding difficult and uncomfortable work or pawning off the work on others. As those who've benefited from systems of oppression, we know we have a responsibility to help dismantle them. We've tried to navigate this tension by drawing from books and other inspirational source materials created by marginalized artists (e.g., *Not Quite Narwhal*) and that support organizations led by marginalized peoples (e.g., 50% of the proceeds from sales of *Fur and Feather Stand Together* go to three nonprofits working towards climate justice: The International Indigenous Youth Council, Center for Biological Diversity, and Sunrise Movement). By doing so, we've tried to center marginalized voices without shirking our responsibility to act toward change.

We also continue to wrestle with how to empower our (majority nondisabled, otherwise privileged) students to see themselves as changemakers without reproducing white, nondisabled savior narratives. While we again cannot pretend to answer this question, we've tried to attend to it through constructing parallel problems that illustrate our and our students' complicity in systems of oppression. For example, in *The Drama of Sprinkles,* our students were complicit in excluding Sprinkles from attending *Frozen Jr.,* as they had not thought about how inaccessible it might be for a unicorn. In *The Drama of Dr. Inkling,* our students had littered the tape that had traveled to the ocean and attached itself to Dr. Inky's tentacles. Through these creative choices, we've tried to help students see themselves not as outsiders, sweeping in to solve social justice problems, but as insiders, deeply entangled with these problems' existence. We've also been intentional about the kinds of stories we tell. While choosing inspirational source material for *The Drama of Dr. Inkling,* we were drawn to *We Are Water Protectors* (Lindstrom, 2020), a beautiful picture book about a young indigenous girl standing up to protect Earth's waters. However, when we considered this story, we struggled to imagine a parallel problem that would result in something other than our (privileged) students "discovering" the importance of protecting Earth's waters, a practice that indigenous communities have understood since time immemorial. Ultimately, we did not feel we could engage this story responsibly, so we chose another direction. Though we have not yet done this for a creative drama, we have also hired cultural consultants to lead lessons that our staff, given our identities, could not appropriately facilitate (e.g., for our 2018 production of *Mulan Jr.,* we brought in two consultants who taught students about elements of Chinese culture). This might be another option for theatres interested in exploring a particular theme, but who lack the lived experiences to do so responsibly. Finally, at the end of our dramas, we've tried to avoid giving our students too much closure. We want them to feel as if they've helped someone navigate systems of oppression, not that they've "solved ableism" or "solved climate injustice." These are pervasive systems; we cannot "solve" them in a four-week summer theatre camp (or perhaps ever). However, we can begin to see ourselves as entangled with these systems and capable of resistance.

## CONCLUSION

To help our summer camp community authentically learn about IDEA issues and resist systems of oppression, PVTC has turned to creative drama adventures. Through multi-episode, interactive stories like *The Drama of Sprinkles* and *The Drama of Dr. Inkling*, our students and staff have learned about systems of injustice, acknowledged our complicity in these systems, and practiced leveraging our agency towards change. We've seen students engage in this critical-consciousness with passion and joy, developing artwork (e.g., the sustainability rap) and begging for more time with our creative drama characters (e.g., Sprinkles' popularity with our Kindergartners). And, our creative drama adventures have supported our other summer camp goal: producing high-quality musical theatre performances with our kindergarten through eighth-grade youth. While we continue to grapple with ongoing tensions, we offer our story in the hopes it might support other nonprofit theatres and theatre educators interested in exploring social justice issues with students but unsure about how to begin.

Nothing that we do as theatre educators will "solve" systems of oppression, but we hope you'll join our students in recognizing how "We can help!" Incorporating creative drama adventures into your existing educational theatre programming might be a good place to start.

## SUGGESTED CITATION

Zdeblick, M.N., and Gibbs, N.G.M. (2024). "We can help!": Using creative drama to explore social justice in youth theatre. *ArtsPraxis, 11* (1), pp. 14-38.

## REFERENCES

Adelman, R. B., Norman, T., & Hamidi, S. Y. (2020). Identity matters. All. The. Time. Questions to encourage best practices in applied theatre. *ArtsPraxis,* 7 (2b), pp. 12–25.

Bailey, S. (2010). *Barrier-free theatre: Including everyone in theatre arts in schools, recreation, and arts programs-regardless of (dis)ability*. Idyll Arbor, Incorporated.

Bailey, S. (2021). *Drama for the inclusive classroom: Activities to support curriculum and social-emotional learning*. Routledge.

Bhukhanwala, F. (2014). Theater of the oppressed in an after-school program: Middle school students' perspectives on bullying and prevention. *Middle School Journal, 46* (1), pp. 3–12.

Bhukhanwala, F., Dean, K., & Troyer, M. (2017). Beyond the student teaching seminar: Examining transformative learning through arts-based approaches. *Teachers and Teaching, Theory and Practice, 23* (5), pp. 611–630.

Boal, A. (1979). Theater of the oppressed. Urizen Books.

Brown, A. (2020). A welcoming space for whom?: Race and inclusion in suburban high school theater programs. *ArtsPraxis, 7* (2b), pp.

132–148.

Cahill, A. J., & Hamel, C. (2022). *Sounding bodies: Identity, injustice, and the voice*. Methuen Drama.

Dunn, K., Luckett, S. D., & Sicre, D. (2020). Training theatre students of colour in the United States. *Theatre, Dance and Performance Training, 11* (3), pp. 274–282.

Dyches, J. (2017). Shaking off Shakespeare: A white teacher, urban students, and the mediating powers of a canonical counter-curriculum. *The Urban Review, 49* (2), pp. 300–325.

Eisner, E. (1998). What do the arts teach? *RSA Journal, 146* (5485), pp. 42–51.

Finneran, M., & Freebody, K. (2015). The liminal space between drama and social justice. In *Drama and social justice: Theory, research, and practice in international contexts*. Routledge.

Freire, P. (1970). *Pedagogy of the oppressed*. Herder and Herder.

Gallagher, K., Starkman, R., & Rhoades, R. (2017). Performing counter-narratives and mining creative resilience: Using applied theatre to theorize notions of youth resilience. *Journal of Youth Studies, 20* (2), pp. 216–233.

Griswold, D. (2020). *Fur and feather stand together*. Orange House Publishing.

Horn, E. B. (2017). "Do you see me?" Power and visibility in applied theatre with black male youth and the police. *Youth Theatre Journal, 31* (2), pp. 79–91.

Lazard, C. (2019). Accessibility in the arts: A promise and a practice. Recess.

Lewis, T. (2022). Working definition of ableism—January 2022 update.

Lindstrom, C. (2020). *We are water protectors*. Roaring Brook Press.

Marín, C. (2007). A methodology rooted in praxis: Theatre of the oppressed (TO) techniques employed as arts-based educational research methods. *Youth Theatre Journal, 21* (1), pp. 81–93.

McAllister-Viel, T. (2021). 'Embodied voice' and inclusivity: Ableism and theater voice training. In *Inclusivity and equality in performance training*. Routledge.

Resene, M. (2017). From evil queen to disabled teen: *Frozen* introduces Disney's first disabled princess. *Disability Studies Quarterly, 37* (2), Article 2.

Sandahl, C. (2005). The tyranny of neutral: Disability & actor training. In P. Auslander & C. Sandahl, *Bodies in commotion: Disability and performance*, pp. 255–267. University of Michigan Press.

Sannino, A., Engeström, Y., & Lemos, M. (2016). Formative interventions for expansive learning and transformative agency. *Journal of the Learning Sciences, 25* (4), pp. 599–633.

Schroeder-Arce, R. (2017). Beyond acknowledgement of whiteness: Teaching white theatre teachers to examine their racial identity. *Youth Theatre Journal, 31* (2), pp. 105–113.

Sima, J. (2017). *Not quite narwhal*. Simon & Schuster Books for Young Readers.

Sins Invalid. (2019). Skin, tooth, and bone: The basis of movement is our people, a Disability Justice primer (second edition). Primedia eLaunch LLC.

Snyder-Young, D. (2011). Rehearsals for revolution? Theatre of the oppressed, dominant discourses, and democratic tensions. *Research in Drama Education: The Journal of Applied Theatre and Performance, 16* (1), pp. 29–45.

Souto-Manning, M., Cahnmann-Taylor, M., Dice, J., & Wooten, J. (2008). The power and possibilities of performative critical early childhood teacher education. *Journal of Early Childhood Teacher Education, 29* (4), pp. 309–325.

Stillman, J., Ahmed, K. S., Beltramo, J. L., Catañeda-Flores, E., Garza, V. G., & Pyo, M. (2019). From the ground up: Cultivating teacher educator knowledge from the situated knowledges of emerging, asset-oriented teacher educators. *Asia-Pacific Journal of Teacher Education, 47* (3), pp. 265–285.

Streeter, J. R. (2020). Process drama as a liberatory practice. *ArtsPraxis, 7* (2b), 79–91.

Syler, C., & Chen, A. (2017). Casting youth/developing identity: Casting and racial and ethnic identity development. *Youth Theatre Journal, 31* (2), pp. 92–104.

Tanner, S. J. (2018). Naming whiteness in a high school drama program: A youth participatory action research, theatrical inquiry into whiteness. In *The Palgrave Handbook of Race and the Arts in Education*.

Troxler, R., Goldstein, T., Holochwost, S., Beekman, C., McKeel, S., & Shami, M. (2023). Deeper engagement with live theater increases middle school students' empathy and social perspective taking. *Applied Developmental Science, 27* (4), pp. 352–372.

Ward, W. (1960). *Drama with and for children*. U.S. Dept. of Health, Education, and Welfare, Office of Education.

We See You W.A.T. (2020).

Whitfield, P. (2022). *Inclusivity and equality in performance training: Teaching and learning for neuro and physical diversity*. Routledge.

Winn, M. T. (2012). The politics of desire and possibility in urban playwriting: (Re)reading and (re)writing the script. *Pedagogies: An International Journal, 7* (4), pp. 317–332.

Zdeblick, M. N. (2023a). Loving critiques of theater education: A DisCrit analysis. American Educational Research Association (AERA) Annual Meeting, Chicago.

Zdeblick, M. N. (2023b). "Play my clip!": Arts-mediated agency in disability-centered learning and research. *International Journal of Qualitative Studies in Education*.


**AUTHOR BIOGRAPHIES**

Maddie N. Zdeblick (she/her) is a teaching artist, theatre director, and PhD candidate in education at the University of Washington Seattle. Maddie is passionate about Disability Justice, educational equity, and innovating new theatrical forms with learners of all ages and abilities. She is also the founding Artistic Director of Parachute Players, a multisensory, immersive theatre company. Maddie holds a master's in education from the University of Washington Seattle and a bachelor's in Theatre and Sociology from Northwestern University, with a focus in Theatre for Young Audiences. She is a 2019 graduate of the Washington State Teaching Artist Training Lab.

Noëlle GM Gibbs (she/her) is an interdisciplinary theatre-maker, educator, and writer living in the San Francisco Bay Area. She is the Executive Director of Portola Valley Theatre Conservatory where she produces plays, musicals, and devised works with community members aged 3-103. Additionally, Noëlle has worked as a freelance director, choreographer, and teaching artist in regional theatres, local nonprofit spaces, and in public and independent schools across California. Noëlle holds dual BAs in Theatre & Dance from UC San Diego and is currently working towards her MFA in Creative Writing at San José State University.

# 'If they can't come to you, go to them': Pivot-Spaces and Kinesthetic Spectatorship in Back Alley Parade Performances for Young Audiences

JAMES WOODHAMS

UNIVERSITY OF EXETER

## ABSTRACT

*The COVID-19 pandemic forced many theatre companies and buildings to reconsider how they approach engagement with audiences (Turner, 2021; Braidswood, 2021). Street performance became one of the go-to choices for reaching audiences and engaging them in a space that was available to practitioners. However, street performances could not guarantee reaching a large audience. Barbican Theatre Plymouth looked to challenge this by bringing a live performance to the homes of a community and young people to engage them in a theatrical event. Back alleys have been a site of historical play since the 1970s (Cowman, 2017) but this has shifted in recent decades. The question arose if this site could be reactivated as a site of play if it would reach a large audience of young people. This article looks to analyze this practice as a research project, looking at the Barbican Theatre Plymouth's second Back Alley Puppetry Parade in June 2021. Building on McKinney's (2013) definition of a scenographic spectacle, this paper argues that the use of a pivot space became vital in establishing a different spectatorship, based on unruliness and kinesthetic experience. It generates ownership as young people choose where they would engage in the performance.*

## INTRODUCTION

Accessibility to theatre and young people engaging with theatre has been on the decline in the United Kingdom since 2009 with a decrease of 23.3% in young people engaging in theatre from 2010–2020 (Statista, 2021). The COVID-19 pandemic held the potential to increase this decline further. The lockdown caused all traditional theatres to close, causing theatre industries' economic turnover in 2020 to drop 90% across Europe compared to 2019, thus causing a reduction equivalent to £32 billion (Lhermitte, 2021, p. 3-4). Due to this, industries and theatres looked at more cost-effective and COVID-safe ways to enable access to theatre and performances. With the potential to reach community safety and even challenge the engagement decline, many companies focused on street performance and alternative open-air performance sites to reach communities. Many companies became key components for many theatre companies to survive the closure of theatre buildings (Giley, 2021). Whilst outdoor performance has always been part of the theatrical ecology (Mason, 1992; Ferdman, 2018; O'Malley, 2018) conditions of the pandemic show greater light on the 'potential to reimagine what 'open-air performance' might be (Turner, 2021).

Clive Lyttle, who directed the Newham Unlocked festival, noted he is a 'big advocate for outdoor arts anyway. It is a democratic way of presenting art. That's one of the things about being able to perform in areas where people don't usually go to theatres' (Braidswood, 2021). Lyttle indicates that performing outside and in public spaces especially means you can directly form a link with audiences that usually do not engage with the theatre. David Calder (2020, p. 324) argues that performance in public space, especially street theatre, relies on the 'suspension or overturning of everyday rules.' Excitement comes from performances in unconventional spaces by changing the use of an everyday space. Using performance to alter how a space is perceived or used can, in Calder's view, draw greater excitement from those engaging. It draws people's eyes and can encourage those who were not actively looking to participate in a theatre event to engage with the performance. Public space performances allow for accidental attendance, increasing the chances of access for communities underrepresented in theatre.

However, audiences are more transient with performances in a public space. Lyttle continues to note that 'when you're in a theatre, you've paid for your ticket and it's noticeable if you get up and leave. Whereas, when you're performing outdoors, the audience can just drift' (Braidswood, 2021). Lyttle argues that performance within a public space does not have the same hold over an audience. They might not have planned to engage with the work or may become distracted by something else. Long-form narratives might work, but you are not guaranteed that audiences will stay for the whole piece and thus receive the payoff from the production. Cordileone and Whorton (2015, p. 300) agree with Lyttle, stating that 'the informality of the proximity eases tensions and promotes an atmosphere of play rather than performance.' Public spaces fundamentally shift the audience experience to something different, something that requires even more engagement, and even more co-creation.

## BACK ALLEYS AS A SITE OF PLAY

For a long time, the back alleys that ran behind Victorian-Edwardian terrace housing were a site of play and socialization. Many families saw these spaces as key places for 'play, or chatting to neighbours', slowly becoming a safe social place for the communities that occupy them (Cowman, 2017, p. 234). Back alleys help generate social networks without having the implications that inviting someone into your house poses. Later in the 20th century, however, with car ownership on the rise, back alleys became threatened as town planning shifted in favour of the car under the name of economic profitability (p. 234). This was coupled with society starting to call children who were playing in their physical space behind their house gutter children or talking about gutter play (Read, 2011, p. 421). Read (*ibid.*, p. 425) argues that many families used this term as they 'were more often concerned with [children's] presence as a theatre, prefiguring their later street lives as thieves and beggars, than with their safety.' Societies of play in back alleys led to children starting not to play in their local space. As priorities shifted to focus on motorization and the growing use of these spaces for refuse storage, the focus changed to moving childhood play to parks or what was termed 'safe play space' (p. 431) leading to a decline of back alleys these traditional play spaces.

Cowman noted (2017, p. 247), however, that back-alley spaces were an important space for mothers and children to socialize and play with their neighbours and friends whilst being close to home. Mothers in different cities fought for the right to create a play street, free from traffic and a place for the children to play safely. This shows that back alleys were always vital public community spaces and place for play. Paul Simpson notes (2011, p. 422) that street performance can and do change 'something to the way people relate to each other, even if this something is only fleeting and ephemeral.' Thus street performances could reactivate the history of play, imagination and community gathering in back-alley spaces. Simultaneously, the back-alley space brings a performance into these spaces to reach young people directly in their homes. It could be a rich performance space in which you could target and challenge access issues for a specific community.

This practice as a research article will analyze how taking performance to back-alleys would generate genuine engagement from young audiences. It aims to investigate if families are interested in being involved in a performance even if it comes to their literal back door. How do creative practitioners enhance a site that is mainly used for refuse into something performative? It uses a case study of the Back Alley Puppetry Parade which took place in Keyham, Devon on the 10th June 2021. A qualitative approach was undertaken for this puppetry parade, using practitioner interviews and audience notes to analyze and understand the creative potential of the back alley as a site of performance.

## METHODOLOGY

Using an exploratory case study methodology, this qualitative paper examines one performance of Back Alley Puppetry to analyze back alleys as a site of performance. As Arya Priya (2021, p. 96) notes, exploratory case studies illuminate 'phenomenon with the intention of 'exploring' or identifying fresh research questions which can be used in subsequent research studies in an extensive way.' Interviews act as the backbone of the methodology, using reflective and rapid response techniques to understand their approach in generating work for a back alley space and their reflections on the performance. Consent for recordings were sought in advance and re-confirmed before the recorded interview. Four fixed questions were used for reflective interviews to gain insight into the creative approach for generating work for this space and considering audience engagement. Follow-up questions were left fluid to allow me as the researcher to respond to queries raised. Each interview lasted between thirty minutes to one hour. These were further supported by rapid response interviews which took place straight after the performance.

Practitioner insights are supported by noted observation and photography of the event. Houses along the parade route were sent both promotional and research information. Further verbal consent was sought from audience members directly and their carers, if applicable, to use certain observations. Where consent was not granted, photos and observation data were either destroyed or not collected.

## BACK ALLEY PUPPETRY PARADES

The original back-alley puppetry parade was a concept I had proposed in the summer of 2020 as a potentially safe performance site to reach communities and was performed in September 2020 in St Jude's, Plymouth, UK. Puppetry has been used in recent history to dimmish separation in defined spaces. Ana Diaz Barriga (2009, p. 146) used giant puppets at the US/Mexico border as the scale of the puppet diminished 'the importance of the border wall and believed puppets could be a useful means to achieve this.' The monumental scale of this puppetry allows to potentially distort spaces, especially space which have been clearly defined be that by a border rule or government rules that define your house as one of the only designated "safe" earlier. The parade combined community members, professional performers, and dancers alongside the creators to generate the event. The creative team, which was the same between the two parades, was led by me as producer and Ruth Webb as lead designer. Multiple other artists contributed to the delivery of the parade including Charlie Ranken as Movement Director, Zenna Tageny as Assistant Designer, Ben Isabel as Junk Band Leader, Chloe Benbow as Jellyfish Designer and Maker, Vick Horan, Finely Newbury, Charlotte Kransmo and Helen Bov as Puppeteers for the event. The parade would walk 2.2 kilometres worth of back alleys, starting the event in the park next to the houses.

**Figure 10:** Back-alley Puppetry Parade Full Cast. Credit: Josh Marsh

**Figure 11:** Parade in Back-alley. Credit: Josh Marsh

Community members made up the majority the performers. Most of these performers were Keyham residents, complemented by young people who engaged in other Barbican theatre activities. Community members were engaged throughout outreach workshops which took place on the 15th and 16th of May 2021. These workshops led to the creation of the prawns for the parade. Within the workshops, community members helped create the prawn design from scratch based on a simple design created by Ruth Webb. Each community member built their costumes. We wanted to give them a sense of ownership over what they were creating and performing, to encourage them to be able to engage in play with performers and spectators.

**Figure 12:** FishGo Disco & Jellyfish Puppets. Credit: Josh Marsh

Further performers came from the ReBels programme, the youth engagement arm of the Barbican Theatre Plymouth. I was the coordinator for these groups and had designed specific topics that would feed into the performance. The first group was focused on puppetry, which ran in Autumn 2020. As the performance was originally meant to take place in January 2021 the group schedule would have concluded with the performance. However, due to the second COVID lockdown which moved the performance, the group had an extra rehearsal scheduled in May to help get them coordinated as an ensemble. The second rehearsal, Junk Band Music, ran from April–July 2021. The puppet parade was their first performance.

The parade was configured in the following order from front to back; *Fish Go Disco* fish, jellyfish, junk band, prawns and finally the seven-metre-tall giant fisherman. Whilst the parade did have a very strict distancing system to ensure alignment with COVID restrictions (including masks as part of all costumes), playfulness was brought in through a non-narrative. Person to person interaction was prioritized to enable creative interplay with spectators. Puppeteers were encouraged to interact and respond to what the spectator offering generating small moments of uniqueness. Street performance is built on flexibility of script as it allows performers to deal disruptions and turn them 'into entertaining diversion' (Harrison-Pepper, 1990, p. 114).

Conversely, as a creative team we wanted singular cohesive moment that brought performance together. This then acts as point of differentiation from the individualistic encounters between spectators and puppets that dominated the parade. The choreographed movement phrase that was performed at unspecified times throughout the parade, launched by a specific drum roll from the band. At this moment, the fisherman called for the parade to hall in the nets, with all sea creatures shouting "No" back to the fisherman. The giant fisherman would then lean forward to try and grab the prawns in front of him. This movement sequence added group cohesion in most of the improvised interactions with spectators along the route as captured in [this video](#).

## DISCUSSION: PREPARING A SITE FOR CREATIVE ACTIVITY

My main concern when first proposing using back alleys as a performance space was how we as practitioners could generate a vibrant enough feeling that challenges the dominant narrative of it being a refuse space. Whilst there is a history of these spaces being used as a site of imaginative play, there has not been a recent history of them as a performance site. The site has been used as an incidental space, where neighbors might greet each other, but no substantive play occurs. It can be both a social space, but it is usually encountered as an individual one. Some streets along the route even had 'No Ball Games' signage as you entered each road. Compounding these issues was the pandemic lockdown itself, which further distanced residents from the back alley as a social space as they complied with lockdown restrictions. At this time, it truly became a site where either people transitioned to their homes or a place to store refuse.

To understand the space, the full production team did six walks of the area, with two extra walks to remove discarded nappies, broken glass and other refuse. Whilst on these walks before the performance we only had one instance of seeing young people playing. Zenna Tagney, design assistant on the project, noted many audience members saw this space as 'their back- alley, which is normally full of junk...they don't think about [it] on a daily basis' (J. Woodhams, Personal Communication, 22$^{nd}$ June 2021). It is a public space that is used by residents mainly as a transition space. It is a place where residents move from one area to another. Figure 4 shows the space had become a space where bins are kept out constantly. The space is a functional extension of the home. Mason notes that many walkabout performances have a great 'disruptive essence' (Mason, 1992, p. 166). Even though the parade itself was transient, it held the potential to subvert the act of transitioning it by adding color, music and giant puppets.

**Figure 13:** Back-alleys of Keyham. Credit: James Woodhams

Walking around the space for the original parade route in September 2020, it became clear that the back-alley occupies a duality that balances between a public and private space. I have named this duality a pivot space. Even if the resident owns or rents, the idea of a home or a home space embodies purely private space. People occupy and behave in their home space very differently than the public spaces. The vast majority of the back-alleys in Keyham are publicly accessible and do not have exclusive access for residents. This makes them a public space in which a different set of norms and behaviors are embodied by people within it (Simpson, 2011; Laurier & Philo, 2006). However, the back-alleys are not purely a public space, as there is an ownership of the space from the houses that back onto it. Cowman (p. 247) indicates these spaces were once seen as an extension of the home, a place of collective gathering. The back-alley space then embodies a pivot space. The communities that owned the houses around it claimed these spaces as their own, thus providing a sense of private space in which a young person has the potential for increased comfort in the space. However, as it is publicly accessible, it still holds some societal norms that you would find in play parks and high streets. The duality of types of space generates greater room for manipulation and change within a space. It became clear the space being so close to people's houses could lead to a dynamic engagement with the right stimuli as the production enters "their space." The pivot space's potential to generate an atmosphere of imaginative inclusivity and openness was an interesting area to investigate.

Seeing this potential within back-alleys enabled a clear approach for the creative team of what theatrical techniques deployed were key to accessing this duality. For both parades, we sought a creative subversive approach to manipulate the space into a site of imaginative play. Laura Kriefman, CEO of Barbican Theatre, noted that the space chosen determined the very nature of the performance itself:

> With the puppets in the back-alley, [the] fundamental thing was being visible over their back fences as much as possible. And therefore, the scale of this thing is massive...that's where I think we started [...] I think [it] is a very interesting way of making, because we are not limiting any of our creatives and any of our young people, we're showing that creative storytelling or creative making is not limited to a nine-by-eight black box. (J. Woodhams, personal communication, 25th May 2021)

Kriefman is arguing using the performance space as the stimuli enabled a production design that would manipulate dimension of the back ally. The space presented the opportunity to choose giant puppetry that could reach over the walls to reach spectators' back gardens or even bedroom windows encouraging the performance to exploit pivot-space features, to actively subvert the space to help play with the public/private tensions that the space holds.

However, we did appreciate this subversion might not have been welcomed without warning. If the performance had just turned up without prior notice, it would have been very disruptive for the residents. Emma Miles points out that for young audiences 'it is not just the performance itself that is significant, but the rituals of theatre-going and the social meanings made by children about and through the theatre space' (Miles, 2018, p. 37-38). Miles argues that the act of theatregoing helps to lay the groundwork for the imaginative experience to occur and for young people to get prepared for the imaginative spectatorship. However, Miles notes that 'our understanding of 'the theatre' is as geographic as it is temporal' (Miles, 2018, p. 28). With theatre associated with a building even if the act can be performed anywhere.

**Figure 14:** ReBels Junk Band. Credit: Josh Marsh

Further to this, if the audience is not going to a production and staying at home, does this affect the ability to build excitement? The creative team thought it was important to generate a sense of theatre-going experience through excitement at the parade coming to the local area. To generate this theatre-going feeling, the practitioners devised three approaches to help ensure the community knew of the performance and how to engage with it.

The first approach was co-creating the performance with the community. Having community investment was vital to the rationale of the performance, a way to celebrate together safely within slowly relaxing COVID-19 restrictions. This meant we could start to embed the performance as community members could see their neighbors perform and give a sense of the upcoming performance. This community focus led to one community performer using the performance to help integrate themselves into the community, even stopping mid-parade from having a chat with their new neighbor.

Marketing ensured the community knew the performance and research would take place. We delivered flyers to every house on the parade route the week of the performance to let them know this was happening, with further posts on community social media pages. This generated excitement and interest from people on social media. The initial advertisement of the parade route even generated some inter-street rivalries, with some community members asking why the parade wasn't coming down their street or asking to come back to their side of the park next time.

Whilst the above measures laid the ground for anticipation, they did not generate that direct excitement of gathering for the experience. To generate this effect, the creative team knew we needed to signal of our arrival intimate arrival to the community. This was both a practical and theatrical choice as it both acted as the call to gather for the performance and warned spectators that the parade was coming down their street, as the advertisement could only offer a start time for the parade. It decided music was needed to help prepare and announce the parade's arrival. Due to this, a Junk Band was formed which was made up of the Barbican Theatre's youth theatre program. Beyond the practical effect of gathering spectators to watch the parade, the band provided performers with a rhythm and energy for the hour of the parade and helped to signal the joint 'haul in the net' moments. To help manage the parade they were placed in the middle to have an equal sound to all performers. The need to increase the sense of a theatre-going event generated a greater richness to the sensory texture of the parade.

## Enabling Individual Spectatorship

Deploying an artistic form that could reach beyond the boundaries of the space helped initiate engagement for young spectators. Figure 6 depicts the way the puppetry took advantage of the pivot space to form an engagement with spectators.

**Figure 15:** Attendees Sat on Garage Roof Interacting with Giant Fisherman. Credit: Josh Marsh

The figure shows how a giant puppet was able to reach some young audience members watching the parade on top of a roof extension. The young audiences are smiling with one reaching for the puppets and others giggling at the sight. This shows the excitement at the strangeness of the theatrical event. As the parade entered the back alley it caused enough intrigue to not only pull families to their windows but for them to want to come closer to the event itself, to appreciate the tactility of the puppet. The puppet was able to bridge the gap between the functional space of the alley with the home space, playing with the pivot-space nature to heighten this theatrical moment. Figure 6 was indicative of many moments of the audience coming to the parade throughout the parade.

Throughout the parade's procession, each spectator chose their view and style in which they engaged the parade. The variety of sites to engage the parade is clearly shown in Figures 7 watching from their windows in their homes.

**Figure 16:** Audience Watching from Home Windows. Credit: Joanna Cann

Figure 8 shows people watching from their back garden wall, being as close to the parade as possible. Laura Kriefman noted that 'it was amazing to see 1,000 people feeling safe and able to enjoy giant performance that came to them, and could reach them at their bedroom windows, their balconies or their back gates' (Giley, 2021).

The act of bringing a performance to the homes of young audiences gave them agency over their spectatorship, allowing each spectator to choose how they would want to engage. This not only provided an accessible safe Covid-19 approach but gave greater flexibility and ownership to individuals in engaging or not engaging with the performance.

This offer to take ownership of their spectatorship led some young audiences to using local knowledge to continue their viewing experience. Charlie Ranken noted that spectators chose to follow the

**Figure 17:** Spectators at Back Door Interacting with FishGo Disco Puppet. Credit: Josh Marsh

parade, 'running between alleyways to get ahead (J. Woodhams, personal communication, 18th June 2021) to see it again. Other spectators chose to first watch in their homes, and then walk to the 'crossroad bits, where there were lots of [spectators] standing and waiting' (J. Woodhams, personal communication, 18th June 2021). These crossroad sections in the parade were usually the spaces where the rehearsed section of the parade was performed. Ranken stated she was surprised at the spectators' desire to come to different sections of the parade to watch more. They said 'it was a bold move. Like, they wanted it, there was this desire to be part of this parade. And I think that comes from like a year and a half of, obviously, being in lockdown and not being able to engage with anything. But again, I think it just comes back to just feeling mentally safe' (J. Woodhams, personal communication, 18th June 2021). Spectators wanted to generate a unique interplay with the puppets and wanted the puppet to respond. This desire, enhanced by the pivot-space nature of the alley, enabled the young people to feel mentally safe to engage with the parade and respond the stimuli it was providing. The pivot-space enabled young people to actively choose how much and where they engage the parade, be that watching from their windows or actively following between streets.

## COMBINING OWNERSHIP AND SUBVERSION

Charlotte Kransmo, one of the puppeteers in the parade, noted that for spectators the spectacle was about 'bringing something like joy and something spectacular to an everyday place' (J. Woodhams, Personal Communication, 10th June 2021). Kransmo's statement acknowledges that the act of bringing a performance to a public space holds the potential to generate greater joy and engagement. Bringing a production to an unconventional space is an act of subversion, reconfiguring what happens in the space for the audience. Ruth Webb, the lead designer of the parade, agrees with Kransmo stating that:

> …by [it's] very nature, [it] will be something that's unusual to face, which is, they have great ownership over it, especially children…we're somewhere where they play and walk down every day, I think they very much have a sense of ownership as a, you know, a street behind their house or street that where they walk to a shop. And suddenly, you've added this whole entire other layer to it. Yes, they're already in their comfort zone...what also works really well in the surprise element, where it's once again, it's that space, and then this event space, [then back to] being what their space always is. And suddenly, their status transforms. So, I think both meet them in a way that hopefully they feel relatively comfortable with. (J. Woodhams, personal communication, 26th April 2021)

Webb is astutely noting the benefits of using a space a young spectator has ownership over enables agency and heighten the usual with an overt colorful stimuli. This agency is enhanced as the performers were actively told to hold individual moments with spectators, to create an interplay with each of them. Being in a young person's home space, a place where they potentially feel comfortable allows them to dictate their experience and their encounter with the performance.

Boel Christensen-Scheel et al (2013, p. 128) agree with Webb noting that productions generate a deep engagement from spectators by 'both respecting and manipulating the exciting physical, social and psychological conditions' of the performance site. Understanding the usual use and conditions of a space, and then designing a production to juxtapose this enables a greater response from residents who are shocked to see their local space being used differently; seeing a site they have ownership over change albeit briefly. Creatives further disrupt the nature of the performance by using puppets that reach over usual boundaries to maximize this engagement. It gave agency to the young person to choose how or where they wanted to engage where they saw fit and with minimal effort. Productions that use a public space that is known by young spectators increase the accessibility for audiences. David Micklem (2021, p. 7) states, 'this work is made for familiar spaces—urban and rural, public and private—it is better placed to respond to the landscapes, environments and the people who live and work within them.' The back-alley space was chosen due to the fact it could engage its audiences from their homes, their gardens, their local corner and their windows. They did not have to move to see the performance, the performance came to them.

Combining the ownership of the space and allowing the young spectators agency in the production gave the young people the confidence to explore a unique creative interplay with the puppets. Figures 9 and 10 depict young people interacting with the giants.

**Figure 18:** Participant Engaging Fisherman Puppet. Credit: Joanna Cann

Each figure shows the young person looking and reaching out to the fisherman puppet, aiming for some kind of connection with it. They both show a different engagement, but a shared joy from being around the parade and the larger than life technique that they have encountered so close to home.

The ability of the giants to form these smaller personal interactions with young spectators impacted their response to the performance. Marc Estein (2010, p. 26) notes that for puppetry to be successful 'many minds are needed...to invent the performance details that make the shows so wonderful.' Engaging with spectators in places in which they already engage their imagination is thus key for spectators to see their giant as full living beings, that are evocative and stir emotion (p.28). These unique interplays were undoubtedly a key factor in the

**Figure 19:** Reaching Up to Fisherman Puppet. Credit: Josh Marsh

enjoyment of seeing, as shown in the figures above. I believe that this agency over the experience could only have been as successful as spectators had ownership of the space. We had designed the production to encourage these types of spontaneous engagement. However, just because the offer was presented to young audiences, did not mean it would be engaged with in this manner. The comfort of knowing space allowed combined with puppets allowed for their responses to be more spontaneous. I believe that to elicit this kind of response in a street performance would require greater amount of offers from the performer. Being in a pivot space, a space they already have a sense of ownership over, enabled a comfortability that enables more spontaneous engagement without persistence from performers. Combination of the pivot space and subversion of the giant puppetry opened accessibility, comfortability and ownership of this different type of spectatorship experience to young person and their family.

## A KINESTHETIC EXPERIENCE

Figures 8, 9 & 10 illustrate how each young spectator was embodying a kinesthetic response whilst embodying spectatorship of the performance. Generating a performance that enhances the nature of a pivot space led us as a creative team to give performers creative freedom to form more spontaneous, natural and creative interplay. This, in turn, generated a different type of spectatorship. Joslin McKinney has described such spectatorship and events as a scenographic spectacle. McKinney (2013, p. 63-64) describes this theatrical experience as a production 'where visual images are the main focus of the audience experience.' McKinney (p. 68) continues to argue that spectacle performances generate an 'intense encounter between individual spectators and the construction [i.e., puppet]' that provides a stimulus for a kinesthetic empathic engagement. Kinesthetic empathy is a way to describe a spectator's engagement that is predominantly a physical response. Dee Reynolds (2012, p. 30) describes this effect in the following way: 'through embodiment, multi-sensory engagement both with the environment and with each other, participants...learned new ways of behaving and new ways of knowing.' The spectacle produces kinesthetic embodied response in response form the performative stimuli physicality within the space.

This embodied response is keenly shown in Figure 11. Figure 11 shows a young spectator and their caregiver being shocked as the giant bends down to them trying to catch them. Before this situation, the young person was calling out to the giant to try and reach him. As it got closer the sheer scale of the giant caused a small fight or flight response, an embodied primal emotion, that caused the spectator to recoil slightly. This then produced a fit of giggles from both spectators. Both spectators indicate pleasure with the playful shock of the giant scale. The joint visceral response increased their enjoyment as they were within the knowledge that they were always safe. It has been noted that 'children need opportunities to do things that are exciting and adventurous...in a safe environment' (Spencer & Wright, 2014, p.

30). Again, the comfortability for the spectator being in their home space, and the performers using pivot space increased the enjoyment of the kinesthetic spectatorship.

The pivot-space environment is a key part of a kinesthetic response. McKinney (2013, p. 70) argues the 'conditions for kinesthetic empathy are based on a tacit and embodied knowledge of the world.' Delivering a production in a space in which young people live day in day enables a greater response to this scenographic spectacle. Bringing in big puppets to an area young people use daily alters their usual kinesthetic experience of that space. The production prompted a different embodiment in the space thus generating a greater imaginative and kinesthetic response. McKinney (p. 74) continues to argue that 'the way a spectacle generates multiple fertile associations,

**Figure 20:** Spectators React to Fisherman Puppet Getting Close to Them. Credit: Josh Marsh

feelings and memories' is 'through unruliness that scenographic spectacle might be capable of deconstructing our relationship to the world at the same time as drawing upon it.' A spectacle provokes an embodied emotive experience based on a shared unruliness. Spontaneous moments and unrehearsed audience interactions based on shared unpredictability enhanced in spectacle through dynamic creative interplay. Ownership of the pivot space intersected with stimuli of the performance to generate a kinesthetic connection between performer and spectator which increases inhibitions to spontaneity laying the foundations for sustained playful encounter.

These conditions led to interactions to become more complex interplays. Performers and young spectators following the parade started to create a game where they and the prawns would go hiding from the giant, and hide behind bins, running behind the giant, pulling faces at the giant and shouting "behind you." These spontaneous games generated a carnivalesque feel to the parade, a joyful unruliness to the production. Comfortability in the space reduced the usual time that 'sort of contact and negotiation to take place' which in turn generates street performance to generate 'a more convivial and sociable form of public space to result' (Simpson, 2011, p. 427). The disruption to the back-alley space with the giant puppet parade and focus on individual engagement allowed for a quicker interplay to form. This interplay was built on unruly playfulness interchange between spectator and performer which holds the potential to increase the memories spectators were generating.

This legacy of the production from this unruly play is shown in Figure 12 which is a social media comment. It speaks to how the parade, even two days after the performance, had a lingering effect on young audiences' imaginations. Through kinesthetic engagement, resisting any form of narrative story, by focusing on the young people's individuality, the spectacle could provide the ability to look at a back-alley space in a different light. It enhanced the anarchic nature of street performance to a new level as a young person change a space they knew intimately. It encourages a young person to start to extend their boundaries of imagination beyond the walls of their home. It allowed them to, albeit briefly, view the back alley of their house as a space of creativity, loud, bright imaginative play at scale.

**Figure 21:** Facebook comment about performance on Barbican Theatre Facebook Page

## CONCLUSION

Back-alleys as a performance space provide a different kind of spectatorship. By reactivating its history as a place of play with a small act of subversion you could provide a performance that enabled a more accessible performance that put the young person's unique creative engagement first. Understanding the restrictive nature of the space, but also appreciating its unique aesthetic of a pivot space enabled a different spectatorship experience. The ability to break over the space through puppetry, prevent offers of spontaneity and be close to a young person's home space increase the creative potential and accessibility of the performance. Being on spectators' home turf, with creatives tapping into the pivot space and the young person connection that they already have with the space and enhanced it. It allowed for a kinesthetic form of spectatorship that could be embodied in the unruly spontaneity that led to a dynamic creative engagement that was individualised. It granted young people greater control over their theatrical experience and gave them agency in a space they might already have agency over.

Whilst responses, figures and analysis indicate to analysis presented here, a limitation of this study would be the lack of direct voices of young people. As this approach focuses on the creative view, a deep understanding would be needed to collaborate with the initial analysis present here. Whilst the performance connected with the past historiography of the site as a place of play to enable a dynamic creative interplay to occur, it could be possible the response was heightened by the months of lockdown that preceded the performance. Due to this, more research should be conducted to analyze if this response is consistent beyond the two lockdown parades conducted by the Barbican Theatre Plymouth. Further research should analyze direct insights from the young people for the performance itself, gathering rapid response data to directly understand the impact of a kinesthetic experience compared to other performance spaces.

Questions also arise on the long-term legacy of the production: how do spectacle productions live in the memory of a young audience would be interesting longitudinal data to analyze.

**SUGGESTED CITATION**

Woodhams, J. (2024). 'If they can't come to you, go to them': Pivot-spaces and kinesthetic spectatorship in back alley parade performances for young audiences. *ArtsPraxis, 11* (1), pp. 39-63.

**REFERENCES**

Braidswood, E. (2021, February 9). The great big get out: Theatres plot open-air comeback for summer. *The Guardian*. Retrieved March 3, 2021.

Calder, D. (2020). Street theatre in a state of exception: Performing in public after Bataclan. *Contemporary Theatre Review, 30* (3), pp. 308-325.

Christensen-Scheel, B., Lindgren, C., Therese Pettersen, A. (2013). Scenography in the staging/ on the stage/ in the mind of the audience. *Performance Research*, *18* (3), pp. 126-143.

Cordileone, A, & Tuggle Whorton, R. (2015). Site-specific theatre: New perspectives on pedagogy and performance. *Research in Drama Education: The Journal of Applied Theatre and Performance, 20* (3), pp. 298-301.

Cowman, K. (2017). Play streets: Women, children and the problem of urban traffic, 1930-1970. *Social History, 42* (2), pp. 233-256.

Diaz Barriga, A. (2019). Beyond the wall: Borderland identity through puppets. *ArtsPraxis, 5* (2), pp. 144-157.

Estrin, M. (2010). The sustainable energy of the bread & puppet theater: Lessons outside the box. *Radical Teacher, 89*, pp. 20-30.

Ferdman, B. (2018). *Off sites: Contemporary performance beyond site specific*. Southern Illinois University Press.

Giley, M. (2021, June 14). Puppets on parade in Keyham. *Plymouth Herald, 19*.

Harrison-Pepper, S. (1990). *Drawing circle in the square: Street performing in New York's Washington Square Park.* University Press of Mississippi, London.

Laurier, E., & Philo, C. (2006). Cold shoulders and napkins handed: Gestures of responsibility. *Transactions of the Institute of British Geographers, 31,* pp. 193-207.

Lhermitte, M. (2021). Rebuilding Europe: The cultural and creative economy before and after the COVID-19 crisis. *Ernst & Young Advisory.*

Mason, B. (1992). *Street theatre and other outdoor performance.* Routledge.

McKinney, J. (2013). Scenography, spectacle and the body of the spectator. *Performance Research, 18* (2), pp. 63-74.

Micklem, D., Basu, S., Chatterton, S. (2021). Outside the conventional and the mainstream: Arts in public spaces in England. *101 Outdoor Arts.*

Miles, E. (2018). Bus journeys, sandwiches and play: young children and the theatre event. *Research in Drama Education: The Journal of Applied Theatre and Performance, 23* (1), pp. 20-39.

O'Malley, E. (2018). "To weather a play": Audiences, outdoor Shakespeare, and avant-garde nostalgia at The Willow Globe. *Shakespeare Bulletin, 36* (3), pp. 409-427.

Priya, A. (2021). Case study methodology of qualitative research: Key attributes and navigating the conundrums in its application. *Sociological Bulletin, 70* (1), pp. 94-110.

Reed, J. (2011). Gutter to garden: Historical discourses of risk in interventions in working class children's street play. *Children & Society, 25,* pp. 421-434.

Reynolds, D. (2012). Mirroring movements: Empathy and social interactions. In Reason, M. & Reynolds, D. *Kinesthetic empathy in creative and cultural practices.* Intellect.

Simpson, P. (2011). Street performance and the city: Public space, sociality, and intervening in the everyday. *Space and Culture, 14* (4), pp. 415-430.

Spencer, K.H. & Wright, P.M. (2014, October 28). Quality outdoor play spaces for young children. *Nutrition and Fitness for All Young Children, 69* (5).

Statista (2023, October 11). *Share of children who participated in theatre and drama activities in the last year in England from 2008/09 to 2019/20, by age.* Retrieved November 8, 2023.

Turner, C. (2021, January 25). And we begin. *Outside the box: Open air performance as pandemic response*. Retrieved January 17, 2022.

**AUTHOR BIOGRAPHY**

James Woodhams is a researcher, theatre-maker, producer and puppeteer based in Plymouth, UK. James has worked across multiple different art forms but specialises in Theatre for Young Audiences and the ways space affects theatrical engagement. He has also worked extensively in community-applied theatre and talent development inside national portfolio organisations. James currently works as a Commercialisation Manager in the Humanities, Arts and Social Sciences department at the University of Exeter, helping researchers turn research outputs into impact at scale.

# Pedagogy, Practice, and Performance: A Practical and Phenomenological Approach with Long Island Classics Stage Company's Classic Kids

DAVID OVERTON

LONG ISLAND CLASSICS STAGE COMPANY

## ABSTRACT

*This is a self-study of the philosophy and processes that comprised the foundation of our theatre company focusing on the inaugural summer theatre intensive program, "Classic Kids." Approaching this account as an Artist/Scholar, this study includes a chronological account of the articulation of a mission statement, workplace values, and questions for inquiry. Further, this documentation then describes selected practices and outcomes that demonstrate the heuristic and phenomenological interchanges that occur during and as a result of these exercises. This self-study further seeks to focus on the transferrable skills developed in performance study to self-actualization in everyday life.*

As a director, actor, playwright, and scholar, I have always been focused on the intersection of performance and everyday living. Much of my practice and theory in performance pursues the question, "How can performance in theatre enhance one's quality of life?" To that end, I created my own performance enterprise called Long Island Classics Stage Company which came into being in the summer of 2012 when I was allowed to use the Community Room on the lower level of Our Lady Queen of Martyrs, a Catholic Church in Centerport, New York, United States of America. The artistic staff included Gina Salvia (a graduate of the New York University, Tisch School of the Arts, who would teach Voice), Rebecca Kupka (Broadway actress, who would teach Dance), and myself (MFA in Acting from the University of North Carolina at Greensboro and Ph.D. in Theatre from the University of Colorado at Boulder) who would teach Acting and Direct the final showcase for an invited audience. The administrative staff included Rebecca and me.

This essay will examine our approach and execution of select aspects of our youth program that existed during the summers between 2012 and 2019. Generally, the narrative will be presented in a chronological order. The essay begins with an account of our founding principles, philosophy, workplace values, and strategies of inquiry. A sample of our exercises incorporated into daily lessons is discussed and parallels between performance pedagogy and living one's everyday life are illustrated. The findings and conclusions include results from a student-centered survey and my own reflections.

To begin, we wanted to devise workplace values and guiding principles that would focus our approach to performance and teaching. After much conversation and deliberation, we articulated how we wanted to recognize our organization by devising our workplace values thusly:

We are:

1. A performance organization: We seek to house a superb ensemble company while frequently soliciting ideas and energies from new members.

2. A teaching organization: We share our knowledge generously.
3. A learning organization: We continually examine and reevaluate our practices to better serve our mission.
4. Collaborators: Partnership is a core business practice, both internally and externally.
5. Inclusive. Ideas, opinions and perspectives are valued in our work.
6. Committed to excellence. We persistently strive for high standards in our work with artists, audience, schools, teachers, students, and each other.
7. Proud of our efforts. We celebrate our successes and take pride in making a difference with our work.

Our guiding principles would determine how we would conceive ideas, content, and lay the foundation upon which we would characterize our company. With our observations and intentions, we tried to encompass all aspects of daily activity and instill a culture of integrity and professionalism. Our guiding principles included the following affirmations:

1. Best performances engender connections that encourage the audience and community to continually reconsider and reevaluate their own perspectives and opinions.
2. Best practices in cultural and community education include the arts as a core component of every person's ongoing learning.
3. Quality comprehensive arts instruction includes opportunities to create, present, and respond to the work of art both individually and collectively.
4. Engaging, empowering, and supporting all stakeholders (the term "stakeholders" is meant to include but may not necessarily be limited to students, classroom teachers, arts specialists, administrators, parents, partner artists, the community) leads to sustained commitment, investment, and learning in and through the arts.
5. At its best, arts instruction is delivered through collaboration among classroom teachers, parents, artists, and art specialists.

6. The most powerful learning occurs when participants are guided toward self-discovery.
7. Ongoing data collection and analysis enables us to recognize, capture, apply, and share our learning amongst ourselves and with others.

With the articulation of both our workplace values and guiding principles, we hoped to convey the seriousness with which we took our work. As many of these points demonstrate, we aimed to connect with a broader constituency than our own institution so that we might become embedded in the community. We were aware of the necessity to connect with area schools and educational professionals, so we developed a focused inquiry question that was inspired from inquiry-based learning and student-centered learning. We determined that education at Long Island Classics Stage Company would be crafted to further educate students and the community about classical plays and Shakespeare, but as a multi-disciplinary art form, it also will serve as a locus for cross-curricular integration. We used the term "multi-disciplinary art form" because we anticipated using visual artists and musicians among our creative team in the conception of performance. Following inquiry-based learning models, we initially constructed our research inquiry as: "To what extent can an instructional program of a performance organization (Long Island Classics Stage Company) intentionally designed to engage the formal curriculum (math, language, social studies, history, science), meta-curriculum (cognitive and learning processes), and the hidden curriculum (social-personal development) leverage increased student learning?" Our hypothesis was that cognitive development increases when explicit connections are made between fundamental concepts and processes shared by performance and:

1. Social/emotional development (hidden curriculum): Self-discipline, self-esteem, tenacity, empathy, self-assessment, peer and parent collaboration, motivation, focus, a love for learning and the stimulation for students to become life-long learners.
2. Math (formal curriculum): Measurement, proportion, patterns, logical thinking, hierarchies, computation.
3. Language (formal curriculum): Character, theme, voice,

decoding of text/performance text/set design, inference, syntax, composition, setting, writing, sequence.
4. Learning processes (meta-curriculum): Memorization, problem finding, problem solving, divergent thinking, self-reflection, systems thinking, analytical thinking, creative thinking, aesthetic awareness.

We set high goals for ourselves. But to determine if any of this was possible, we needed an inaugural class of students or an institution and a teacher with whom we could collaborate.

Our first efforts to develop programming involved many meetings to determine how best to begin. After a number of ideas were presented, a three-week summer theatre intensive program seemed to be the most strategic means to create a lab to implement our ideas and pedagogy while drawing interest, and recruiting young talent and prospective investors. We resolved that there would be no audition-for-acceptance process; rather, any student between the ages of seven and seventeen would be admitted so long as they accepted and endorsed the philosophy of our organization as iterated here:

It is the Mission of Long Island Classics Stage Company to present meaningful performances and entertainments not only to delight but to explore pertinent ideas and questions that may build and strengthen our community with an awareness and incorporation of the multicultural people that make up our families, our community, our country, and our world within an environmentally sound and sustainable context. The Long Island Classics Stage Company will conduct itself in ways that promote respect for everyone and provide a safe platform from which artists, educators, and instructors may creatively and uniquely express their views and ideas. The Long Island Classics Stage Company will provide opportunities for underrepresented groups to utilize our facilities for their performance purposes within the parameters of this, our Mission and Vision Statement. The Long Island Classics Stage Company will strive to inspire the desire for learning, for the exploration of ideas, cultures, and community through Educational Outreach programs. Our classes will be designed to motivate students toward the pursuit of truth and artistic excellence, to prepare them for future artistic opportunities and service to the performing arts and the world. The faculty within the Long Island Classics Stage Company will teach in ways that empower, enable, encourage, and understand the wants, needs, and challenges that face today's people of all ages.

As conceived, our Mission and Vision Statement was meant to exist as a living document; that is, it was created with the understanding that it would be subject to continual revision to best meet the needs of our students, faculty, community, and all other constituents.

Next came the question of content. As inspiration, I drew from Harold Bloom's bestselling book (1998), *Shakespeare: The Invention of the Human*, wherein he asks, "The answer to the question 'Why Shakespeare?' must be 'Who else is there?'" (p. 1). We wanted a well-established, venerated playwright and Shakespeare was a logical choice to us. We considered Lope de Vega (1562–1635) who wrote more than 1,000 plays. His themes of love and romance, honor and reputation, fate and fortune, power and politics are indeed worthy, but the general body of his work tends to have limited representation, formulaic construction, and a lack of complexity. We also considered Molière (1622–1673), whose plays with their social commentary, humor and wit, was certainly a consideration, but also lack psychological depth, have limited representation, and repetitive themes and plots. By our estimation, a professional in theatre need only review a few of Shakespeare's plays to surmise that his language, his ability to empathize and take on differing perspectives, opportunities for creative embodiment and imagination provide both breadth and depth for exploration and discovery. Indeed, we felt that working on Shakespeare's plays would offer a multifaceted learning experience that might enhance language skills, foster critical thinking, promote cultural understanding, nurture empathy, develop performance skills, encourage interdisciplinary connections and more. By choosing Shakespeare, we felt secure that the strongest possibility for a transformative journey seemed to await the student.

Coupled with my own appreciation for Shakespeare and education, I had to agree with Bloom, and so began crafting the first classes that our company would present under the heading we called "Classic Kids." Within Classic Kids, we would offer classes in Acting, Dance, and Voice focusing on material that could be considered "classic" within its context. This proved awkward for the Voice and

Dance sections since the material that would be considered "classical" (e.g., opera, ballet) would be unsuitable for the beginner or novice student. We therefore used the term 'classic' in a relaxed context in those two arenas so that the material would include songs and styles of dance from Broadway musicals of the middle part of the twentieth century. By doing so, we allowed ourselves material that parents would be familiar with, and students could be successful in performing. However, with Acting, I resolved the term could be more strictly applied since Shakespeare and the Greek playwrights could be made accessible to the young performer, especially since the intention all along was to use excerpts from plays and musicals rather than attempt a fully conceived production. Further, Shakespeare and the Greek playwrights would add a level of integrity and credibility that we wanted to be connected with our theatre. Since this determination regarding the Acting component most closely embraced the mission and vision of our program, this study will focus on the articulation of this aspect of the program.

While the students were placed into three groups by age (7 to 9, 10 to 12, 13 to 15), the approach to my teaching was consistent in content but varied in delivery. The first guidelines that were applied universally to all the Acting classes came by way of my experience with numerous teachers of improvisation who, of course, learned these guidelines from their mentors. According to Anthony Frost and Ralph Yarrow's findings (1989), these rules may have originally come down from Stanislavski, Meyerhold, Viola Spolin, Jacques Lecoq, and many others, but the precise credit for their origin is impossible to ascertain. Regardless, the three guidelines were as follows: 1. Say the first thing that comes to your mind. 2. Always say, 'Yes! And...'. 3. Make your partner look good. These guidelines provided an effective foundation for all the work we would do in our classes and in the showcase. However, it was the ability to apply these guidelines in everyday contexts that made me realize their real value. For, as I came to learn, these guidelines, when applied to everyday contexts, could exponentially impact the positive development of one's own personal development and interactions with other people.

Consider the application of these guidelines in class during the first days through improvisation. With each class separately, I had the students sit in a circle so that we might begin introductions and facilitated a sharing session. After I explained the guidelines, I asked the students to share three aspects of who they are by sharing their name, grade, and something about themselves of which they are proud. By remembering guideline number 1 (to say the first thing that comes to your mind), the student was required to say whatever sprang to mind. The first two aspects of what they were to share were readily given, but students would often pause before sharing something that made them proud. Whenever this occurred, I reminded the student to share whatever initially sprang to mind. I offered that it could be that they are proud of having perfect attendance at school, that they got an A in Math, that they executed a cartwheel, or anything whatsoever that put a smile on their face. Occasionally, the student's response would be simply to try to elicit a laugh, but rather than call them out on that approach, I waited until everyone had a chance to speak. After we had completed the circle, I gently drew the students' attention to the times when certain students gave a response that was intended to provoke a laugh. I warned the students that this kind of approach is not an effective way to develop as a performer or a person in everyday life. Just as the audience will identify what you did as a deliberate attempt at humor—and thus disengage from the performance—so, too, will other people see the flatness of what you're offering and not think highly of your contribution.

The second guideline was employed whenever we worked within improvisation and a person was given an opportunity to respond. The response should always be, "Yes! And…" meaning that if someone asks you about your daily bicycling routine, you are to respond, "Yes, and I cycled twice as far and picked up milk!" rather than, "No, I don't cycle" which negates the first person's offer and shuts the scene down. Borrowing from Husserl's (1913) idea of "bracketing," this type of approach acts on a phenomenological level and prompts students to abandon preconceived notions and/or prejudices (unfortunately, there is no positive Husserlian definition of "bracketing" or "epoché" as it was originally articulated). In the mode of "bracketing," the student temporarily suspends their natural attitude towards the world, including assumptions, beliefs and preconceptions, and is encouraged to focus solely on the immediate phenomena as they appear in consciousness. The intention is to create a context wherein the student becomes more able to contribute quickly, honestly, and in a manner that is genuinely truthful. When, on the other hand, an actor has a moment to think about their response, the outcome tends to be calculated, flat and uninteresting. One of the aims was to encourage a kind of creativity in expression in the moment that could be transferred to most people in everyday situations. In retrospect, it was this kind of transaction that seems congruent with the way that the Creative Thinking Framework distinguished between "Big C" creativity and "little c" creativity (OECD, 2019). "Big C" creativity demands that "creative thinking be paired with significant talent, deep expertise and high levels of engagement in a particular area" (OECD, 2019, 8). On the other hand, "little c" creativity "does not relate to masterpieces or genius inventions, but is the kind of everyday creativity [that] can be achieved by nearly all people capable of engaging in creative thinking" (OECD, 2019, 9).

The third guideline that was to be used whenever someone appeared to simply go blank or appeared to be struggling in an exercise: make your partner look good by creating more offers, providing more information, or addressing the context. No one likes to feel embarrassed or uncreative and by employing all of these guidelines, all participants in any acting exercise should feel successful.

After the icebreaker exercise, we tried improvisational exercises. These particular improv exercises were fundamental kinds of arrangements so that even the most inexperienced student could participate and make connections. They were to pretend they were moving through water, fire, air, mud, slime, spider's webs, and as heavy, weightless, and so on. All of the classes experienced this approach so that they were all brought to a common understanding of how they might use their voices and bodies in performance. It was in the afternoon when all the students were together that I could review the lessons with everyone and go further.

To begin, I simply had all of the students walk around the space which was very large; about 14,000 square feet. I played music by select artists including Steve Reich (*Music for 18 Musicians*, 1976), Philip Glass (*Glassworks*, 1981), Michael Torke (*Tahiti*, 2011), and similar composers. As the students walked, I initially had them focus on their breath then drew their attention to various parts of their body to try and identify any tension they might be holding; to simply acknowledge it, breathe into it, and don't judge. "Notice what you notice, see what you see," I'd say. Next, I asked them to notice objects around the space. There was no lack of items to choose from since the students had piled their backpacks and lunch boxes along a wall. After they had examined the space, I had them begin noticing each other as they walked. Again, "Notice what you notice, see what you see," I'd say. The approach was deliberately heuristic, and whether the students could discern this or not was inconsequential. I urged them not to make faces or try to laugh or pass any sort of judgment as they looked at one another. Talking was disallowed. Every now and again, I would remind the students that they were looking at other people saying aloud: "These are other people in this program. They have some of the same interests you have. They are just other people on the planet sharing space." The idea was to engage with other people in a non-judgmental, neutral manner. After a few minutes of that, I had everyone stop where they were, close their eyes, and take a deep breath. I had them repeat after me: "Here we are (students repeat). We are here (students repeat). Are we here (students repeat)? Indeed, we are (students repeat)." One more deep breath, and then I instructed them to continue walking.

As they walked, I explained aloud in a steady, measured fashion, that "performance is a collaborative endeavor. Performance is a way of understanding the larger world around us. Performance transcends the ordinary and allows you to be extraordinary. But first, you must make connections with yourself and with others." With those words, I instructed the students to make 2- to 3-second eye contact with as many people as they could as they walked around the space. After a few moments of this, I had students give each other "high fives" then "low fives," then fist bumps. I instructed the students to drop that part of their connecting and simply walk, then walk faster, then to come face to face with a partner in "10, 9, 8..." until I reached one, and "freeze!" They froze and they all had at least a hint of a smile on their face. It is natural for students to seek out other students with whom they have a connection or relationship—which in many cases only occurred earlier that day—and many used this opportunity to get with a 'familiar' partner. But this, of course, was not the goal. I allowed the students to call this arrangement, "partner 1." As they stood face to face, I told them, "Smile at one another! Introduce yourself to your partner, even if you already know them. Wave goodbye and begin walking again." They did so.

It was obvious that the students were enjoying this simple exercise and when I began talking and using some of the same language, they readied themselves for what they thought was coming.

I modified my instructions stating, "This time, I want you to find a different partner in 5, 4, 3, 2, 1, and freeze!" They froze, but this time, they weren't quite as sure. "Notice what you notice, see what you see," was my mantra. The fact that they were not quite as comfortable with their current partner didn't go unnoticed by the students. Like before, I told them, "Smile at your partner! Tell your partner your name! Say, 'I'll see you again!'" They repeated the last part of my instructions, and I sent them walking again. I continued to get them to connect with as many of their peers as I could. The point became clear that they were to take risks, get out of any comfort zone, and accept people for who they are, as they are.

All of the exercises were concluded with a debrief. To begin, I had all the students sit in a large circle. I then asked them to take a deep breath and think about the exercises we had just completed. One by one, I asked students to share how they were feeling or what they were thinking using only one word. Again, this goes back to the first rule of saying the first thing that comes to mind. I am always reminded in these moments how efficient the students become in articulating with greater precision how they feel and/or what they are thinking. The students were, in effect, teaching one another through the heuristic learning they had been exposed to.

In preparation for the next classes in the coming days, I gave all of the students a short quote by Shakespeare that they were required to memorize. For example, some quotes (all taken from The Riverside Shakespeare, 2nd edition) included:

"You that are old consider not the capacities of us that are young." (*Henry IV, Pt. 2*)

"Sit by my side and let the world slip. We shall ne'er be younger." (*The Taming of the Shrew*)

"How many goodly creatures are there here!" (*The Tempest*)

"You blocks, you stones, you worse than senseless things!" (*Julius Caesar*)

"Take note, take note, O world! To be direct and honest is not safe!" (*Othello*)

"The night has been unruly." (*Macbeth*)

On the second or third day of this kind of "walking around the space" exercise, I asked students to begin developing a character. To do so, I had them lead with different parts of their body, such as their jaw, elbow, ankle, even buttocks; first subtly, then grandly. Along with the physicality of their new-found character, they were instructed to speak aloud the Shakespearean line they had been assigned to learn. I called this an "embodiment." Suddenly, the students realized they had created a character on their own.

On a phenomenological level, the students were experiencing anew their own physicality and embodiment of a character. In the moment, they were heuristically developing their character independently. This is to say that insofar as the students are able, they experimented with their own body free from presuppositions or premeditative outcomes. Of course, I instructed the students to consider tempo and pacing both with their physicality and their delivery of text which further enriched their one-person performance. To free themselves of the character they just created and to bring them back to a more neutral state, I had them drop the character and walk as themselves.

When I surmised that they were ready to experiment with another creation, I had them lead from a different part of their body, to find a partner in "5, 4, 3, 2, 1, and freeze!" The students' odd, contorted shapes elicited giggles, of course, but their focus was excellent. I then told the students that they were going to have a conversation with their partner using only the Shakespearean text they had been assigned. I assured them that it doesn't necessarily need to make sense; in other words, after one person speaks, the ensuing response may not seem appropriate but to think of their conversation as rhetorical observations. One can imagine an eight-year-old boy saying, "These are not natural events; they strengthen from strange to stranger," and a twelve-year-old girl using as a reply, "Why are you grown so rude? What change is this, sweet love?" and the exchange working as a micro-scene. Indeed, the students were delighted with their exchange coupled by the shape of their bodies that they had created.

The next goal was to be able to bridge this work on a heuristic level with scene work and eventually a full production, but a full production of any one Shakespearean play was not the focus of this program. To that end, we revisited improvisational work. One of the most valuable and directly relatable improvisational exercises is one called "The Bean Scene" which is an improvisational game that probably has its roots in Viola Spolin's work but has been modified and amended by many theatre practitioners (Spolin, 1963). It is an effective tool that acts as a heuristic device for student learning. This exercise involves one chair and three people who use the following dialogue as a script for their performance.

> PERFORMER A (*seated in the chair, stirs with an imaginary spoon a giant pot of beans*): Oh, it's a lovely day and I'm making beans.
>
> PERFORMER B (*knocks at the imaginary door by pounding on the floor*): Hello? Is anybody home?
>
> PERFORMER A: Oh, yes! Come on in!
>
> PERFORMER B (*enters*): What have you got there?
>
> PERFORMER A: Beans! I'm making beans!
>
> PERFORMER B: Can I try some?
>
> PERFORMER A (*offers a spoonful of beans*): Why, yes! Of course!
>
> PERFORMER B (*eats*): Mmmm! These beans are tasty! (*dies*)
>
> PERFORMER A: Oh, no! She/he's dead! Is there a doctor in the house?
>
> PERFORMER C (*enters from other side of stage*): Why, yes! I'm a doctor! What seems to be the trouble?
>
> PERFORMER A: She/he's dead!
>
> PERFORMER C (*examines* PERFORMER B): Yep. Indeed she/he's dead. Wait a second! She died of bean poisoning!
>
> END SCENE

The dialogue need only be approximated; the sequence and the sense of the story having a beginning, middle, and end are more important. If anyone every forgot a line or appeared unsure, guideline number three was to be employed: Make your partner look good! To get a sense of how the scene works, I had three volunteers go through the scene. Of course, as it is written (or repeated), it's not very interesting. The goal was to take the one of the embodiments they had created in the "walking around" exercise and apply it to the scene. To ensure that the scene would take on a grander sense of performance, I had the students perform the scene using a variety of contexts and genres which might include doing the scene as if you are underwater; as a spaghetti Western; in gibberish; as if you are ninjas; secret service agents; intoxicated; and so on. For an added twist, I occasionally had students perform the scene backwards. This exercise proved invaluable as a means to quickly access a variety of characters. Although they all used the same material, each improv exercise was unique.

The extent to which this kind of work can be applied in other arenas, whether they be artistic, managerial, conceptual, and beyond, is virtually limitless. Isn't this what we, as directors, do whenever we conceive of a new production by Shakespeare or the classical playwrights? While directors and dramaturgs often make cuts to Shakespearean and classical texts, we are still essentially 're-skinning' each production with different actors, costumes, sets, and other design elements. This is not unlike what happens when businesses compete with other similar businesses. Consider the restauranteur who wishes to create a chain of restaurants with Mexican inspired offerings. There will likely be tacos, burritos, enchiladas, and other foods typically associated with Mexican restaurants. Here, the "text" is "Mexican food"; but it's how the food item is prepared, delivered, and in what context that sets each Mexican restaurant apart from Chipotle, Moe's, Qdoba, and others. The structure of the improv game becomes apparent and here we have a bridge between conceptualization in the arts that is not unlike conceptualization in business. This structure can be seen in any number of other businesses who offer similar material. Consider the practices of Google, AOL, Yahoo, Hotmail, and any other email provider. Each platform is delivering a similar service or "text" and yet they have their own unique characteristics in the execution of those services. But again, it's in the delivery of similar texts that sets them apart and makes one more desirable than the other. While this pedagogy is hardly the kind that will produce nuanced performances and actors-as-artists, it is an efficient and direct means of accessing creativity in varied contexts with inexperienced performers.

I decided to apply this concept to scene work using a scene from Shakespeare's *Richard III* when the two murderers are sent to kill Clarence who is lodged in the tower in Act I, scene iv. While this scene is often played seriously, the ability to push it into comedy is easy; but of course, in order for it to be comical, it must be played seriously. Just as we performed the Bean Scene with a variety of genres and contexts, we did likewise with the two murderers' scene. The students developed strong characters with believable physicality and the realization that their words must be clear in order for the comedy to work. Perhaps more importantly, the students' focus during the exercise was heightened to such a degree that they were able to transcend any self-consciousness that would have otherwise inhibited their performance. Under these conditions, states of "flow" and creativity emerge. Moreover, through the utilization of heuristic approaches, students can access the mental and creative latitude necessary to serve as a catalyst for their transformation into Artists. This is not to discount the utility of systematic, highly structured, or algorithmic approaches. Instead, it argues that freedom and embracing failure positively facilitate a type of growth that may mitigate judgment, criticism, and other impediments. The intentionality of the exercise does not necessarily need to be articulated before beginning the work. Indeed, intentionality is achieved simply by the students' acute interest in the exercise itself which leads to a more meaningful experience overall.

During the summer theatre intensive, there were many other improvisational exercises and lessons, but they are too many to enumerate and describe. The goal, as mentioned earlier, was to empower students to use skills developed in performance and transfer those skills to everyday life. The guidelines used for improvisation were readily transferred to everyday life. For example, when students were asked to help around the house, I urged them to say to their parents, "Yes! And…" which would include, "Yes, and I'll take out the garbage on my way to the bus stop!" However, I warned that guideline number one—of saying the first thing that comes to mind—might have to be modified to "say the first *constructive* thing that comes to mind." One student remarked that she had to stop herself from replying to her father, "Yes, and you don't forget to go to the gym today and lose some weight!" which, she admitted, was certainly the first thing that came to her mind. The third guideline, to make your partner look good, meant that the student should consider members of their family and other loved ones in the 'partner' role. When, for example, a brother, sister, or parent asked the student to be patient, they were to do so and, as the guideline states, "Make your partner look good."

To assess the effectiveness of skills transferred from performance to everyday life is extremely difficult since it would be unrealistic to try and track students' decisions and actions from day to day. Still, we drafted a survey seven years after our inaugural summer theatre program to assess the effectiveness of our program which included five prompts focused on the students' confidence in engaging with Shakespeare's text and five prompts focused on their interpersonal skills (data from our survey, 2019). Approximately 200 students were surveyed and 120 surveys were submitted. For each prompt, responders could select one of six options: strongly agree, agree, neither agree nor disagree, disagree, strongly disagree, or not applicable. These were the prompts:

1. As a former student of Classic Kids, I look forward to studying plays by Shakespeare.
2. As a former student of Classic Kids, I am more confident when approaching texts by Shakespeare.
3. As a former student of Classic Kids, I find that studying Shakespearean plays is more enjoyable.
4. As a former student of Classic Kids, I am able to more fully describe characters in Shakespearean plays.
5. As a former student of Classic Kids, I am able to more fully understand the plot in Shakespearean plays.
6. As a former student of Classic Kids, I feel more confident speaking within group situations.
7. As a former student of Classic Kids, I am more confident leading within group situations.
8. As a former student of Classic Kids, I am able to respond more empathetically to other students.
9. As a former student of Classic Kids, I am able to contribute positively within my family.

> 10. As a former student of Classic Kids, I am able to interact with other adults more confidently.

Of the 120 students who responded, more than 90% selected either "Strongly agree" or "Agree" for all questions.

Our hopes for Long Island Classics Stage Company to find investors willing to build a replica of The Globe Theatre came to an end when COVID-19 caused a global lockdown. All performances and classes were canceled, and basic necessities became everyone's focus. Creativity and self-actualization—levels that appear in the highest realms of Maslow's Hierarchy of Needs (1943)—could no longer be goals under these conditions; rather, humanity was collectively constrained to the lower regions of Maslow's pyramid (physiological and safety needs). These conditions were unsustainable for our theatre enterprise and the project has since been indefinitely suspended. Still, our philosophy and goals remain intact. We maintain our belief in the transference of theatrical performance principles to the cultivation of a poetics for everyday life—a pathway towards improved behavior, disposition, and experiences.

While there are many other summer theater programs conducted annually, we believe that ours is set apart from the others because of the philosophy and approach that we used. Other summer theater programs tend to focus on the end-product, something that parents can see and use as confirmation that their money was well-spent. Summer theater programs that produce a single performance piece at the end of their programming like *Grease* or *The Wizard of Oz* have the advantage of being able to advertise a professional looking end-product by using a licensed poster with which most parents will be familiar and thus curb possible dissatisfaction in the overall experience. Indeed, the students who attend these kinds of summer theater programs enroll in the hopes of landing the role of Sandy or Danny in *Grease* and Dorothy or the Scarecrow in *The Wizard of Oz*; but there can only be one Sandy or one Dorothy and thus dozens of disappointed students will be relegated to the supporting roles of High Schoolers or Munchkins. These sorts of systematic and structured approaches are antithetical to our intention of an heuristic approach to actor training.

In the end, learning and understanding are about widening the scope of relevancy for students. Art-making as research inquiry is notoriously ambiguous and ephemeral. Still, applied practices such as those employed in performance-making can be made more appealing when they are successfully connected to real-world application, but to quantify the degree of success is notoriously difficult. The pedagogical and philosophical approaches outlined in this article are intended to be reproducible and adaptable across cultures and identities. The dialectic exchange between performance-making and an actualized self requires an ongoing dialogue between one's creative expression and personal development. Subsequent documentation and quantifying such data require long term study beyond the scope of this examination. Nevertheless, through the process of creating and embodying characters or narratives, individuals can engage in crucial self-discovery and reflection, which allows individuals to explore different facets of their identity, confront internal conflicts, and evolve their understanding of themselves and the world around them. Learning that endures requires refresher courses and professional guidance supports the idea that learning is a continuous journey that extends throughout one's lifetime. It is worth re-stating that knowledge acquisition is not static but dynamic, requiring regular reinforcement and support to maintain proficiency and relevance. Ultimately, theatre practitioners must identify their purpose or purposes for intentionality to occur such that empowers all participants and constituents toward the creation of inclusive and equitable spaces, and by extension, reaches in to real-world application.

## SUGGESTED CITATION

Overton, D. (2024). Pedagogy, practice, and performance: A practical and phenomenological approach with Long Island Classics Stage Company's classic kids. *ArtsPraxis, 11* (1), pp. 64-82.

## REFERENCES

Frost, A., & Yarrow, R (1989). *Improvisation in drama*. St. Martin's.

Glass, P. (1981). Opening. On *Glassworks* [CD]. New York, Dunvagen Music Publishers.

Husserl, E. (2002). *Ideas* (W. R. Boyce, Trans.). Routledge. Original

worked published 1952.
Johnson, D., & Young, J., (Eds.). (1997). *The Riverside Shakespeare*. Houghton Mifflin Company.
Organisation for Economic Co-operation and Development (OECD). 2019. *PISA 2021 creative thinking framework: Third draft*. Paris: OECD.
Reich, S. (1978). Pulses. On *Music for 18 Musicians* [CD]. New York, ECM.
Spolin, V. (1963). *Improvisation for the theater: A handbook for teaching and directing techniques*. Northwestern University Press.
Torke, M. (2011). Fiji. On *Tahiti* [CD]. London, Ecstatic Records.

**AUTHOR BIOGRAPHY**

David Overton is a professor, playwright, and the founder of Long Island Classics Stage Company in Centerport, New York where he primarily works with students on performing the works of Shakespeare and developing transferable life skills. He has over 25 years' of experience teaching high school and college-aged students and is currently a Visiting Professor at Farmingdale State College in the English and Humanities Department. David holds his MFA in Acting and Ph.D. in Theatre and is especially interested in Embodiment and Physical Theatre. His published plays can be found at [Theatrical Rights Worldwide](#).

# Enhancing Critical Thinking Skills and Ethical Responsibility in UK Higher Education in Times of "Polycrisis": Two Case Studies from Drama and Theatre Arts

## ELLEN REDLING

UNIVERSITY OF BIRMINGHAM

## ABSTRACT

*In this uncertain age of "polycrisis," where various types of crises—such as climate change, the refugee crisis, financial instability, wars—intersect in such intricate ways "that the overall impact far exceeds the sum of each part" (World Economic Forum, Global Risks Report, 2023), it is more important than ever to help students look beyond the university walls and address such complexities. This article argues that combining the enhancement of critical thinking skills, which are often linked to rational distancing, with the promotion of ethical responsibility through an affective closeness towards a topic at hand, is a crucial pedagogical approach in UK higher education today. This is because we live in an age which requires both critical analysis amidst, for instance, the rise of 'fake news,' and affective closeness due to, for example, the emotional numbness often caused by the amount and complexity of the crises we are confronted with today.*

*Adding an affective dimension to a more rational approach furthermore has the benefit of encouraging deep learning as opposed to so-called "surface learning" (Race, 2007, p. 36), as an affective encounter/event can bring with it greater attention (Tomkins, 1995) and a longer-term consolidation in one's (bodily) memory (Shouse, 2005). More sustainable and longer-term thinking in the face of complex and lasting crises is crucial particularly in light of largely short-term, election-focused political (in)action and fast-changing news cycles. To illustrate such an interlinking of distancing strategies with pedagogies of closeness, two particular case studies from Drama and Theatre Arts will be analysed because these can effectively highlight the usefulness of this two-pronged approach through their own combination of artistic nearness to 'real-life' socio-political issues as well as artistic distancing.*

## INTRODUCTION

When reporting on the current decline of the arts and humanities at UK universities caused by a governmental focus on the supposed economic "value" of subjects in recent years, newspaper items rightly deplore that this brings with it a loss in critical thinking skills (cf., for instance, Williams, 2024). However, aside from actually adding financial value to the British economy via the creative industries (Universities UK, *Letter to the Prime Minister*, 2024), the arts and humanities, and particularly Drama and Theatre, crucially work on an affective, as well as critical, level. Referring to the 1990s "in-yer-face" playwright Sarah Kane's work, the actor Catherine Cusack, for example, points out that seeing acts of violence directly in front of oneself onstage, enacted "with authenticity" (2013, p. xi), can be far more visceral than reading/watching them, "[a]t arm's length," e.g. via a news report (*ibid.*). Furthermore, working in a visceral way can confront the audience with an "ethical challenge" (Nevitt, 2013, p. 58). In her 1974 performance *Rhythm 0*, performance artist Marina Abramović, for instance, surrounded herself with objects "ranging from a feather, a rose and some honey to a scalpel, a gun and a bullet. She then remained impassive in the space for six hours, during which the spectators were free to do what they wished with her and with the objects" (*ibid.*, p. 57). A lack of reflecting such ethical-affective potential of theatrical works through pedagogical means would be equally as detrimental in turbulent times as would a neglect of critical thinking skills. This is because being *dis*affected often means one remains inactive in the face of problems rather than willing to take helpful action.

In an age of crisis and within divisive times, it is increasingly necessary to let university students encounter and weigh up opposing views, not only in order to encourage them to think critically about these differing options and potentially take sides, but also to (re-)discover the significance of nuance and complexity. Divisiveness, especially online, also often brings with it easy outrage and entrenched opinions. This is why I wanted to specifically look at the emotion of anger in relation to opposition in my third-year undergraduate module on "Theatre, Philosophy and Emotion." With the help of two different philosophies—one ancient, one modern—we discussed the role of anger in Revenge Tragedies such as Seneca's *Thyestes*, and also aimed to affectively engage with incidents of anger online and in "real life" today, using a combined critical-affective pedagogical approach. This example, and one other case study, will be examined in the second part of this paper, after analysing various meanings of—and interconnections between—"critical thinking" and "ethical responsibility" in further detail and exploring why such skills are particularly threatened today and therefore need to be preserved and enhanced.

## THE ROLE OF CRITICAL THINKING SKILLS AND ETHICAL RESPONSIBILITY IN UK HIGHER EDUCATION TODAY

The benefits of supporting higher education students in enhancing their critical thinking skills and ethical responsibility are manifold, both within and beyond university life. Such skills help students to think and act in a more reflective and responsible way, not only in their university course, but also as graduate professionals and global citizens. The current trend amongst UK universities to emphasise so-called "graduate attributes" seems to indicate a wish to help students become more rounded human beings by the time they leave university and thus appear to go beyond mere short-term utilitarian goals. Such attributes—which students are meant to display by the time they graduate—include:

> [C]ritical thinking skills, such as intellectual curiosity, analytical reasoning, problem-solving and reflective judgement; effective communication; leadership and teamwork skills; research and inquiry skills; information literacy; digital literacy; personal attributes such as self-awareness, self-confidence, personal autonomy/self-reliance, flexibility and creativity; and personal values such as ethical, moral and social responsibility, integrity, and cross-cultural awareness. (Hill *et al.*, 2016, p. 156)

As can be seen from this list, these features particularly also foreground critical thinking skills and ethical responsibility. However, amidst growing financial and market pressures faced by the higher education sector (Cribb & Gewirtz, 2013), which threaten to result in an emphasis on *employable* graduates above anything else, universities arguably need to be careful that this does not remain just a superficial and tokenistic approach, but is fully reflected in the curriculum content and pedagogies.

In an age of "polycrisis," which is marked by high levels of complexity, instability and uncertainty, the enhancement of skills and values that reach beyond university life itself, such as critical thinking skills and ethical responsibility, is required more than ever. An era of "liquid modernity" (Bauman, 2000), age of "fragility" (Stehr, 2001) or "risk" (Beck, 1992) was already pronounced in the 1990s/early 2000s, but in recent years this seems compounded by the sheer number of—and intricate intersections between—the challenges the world is currently faced with. As historian Adam Tooze explains, "polycrisis" is a term that signals the destabilising experience of being confronted with numerous and varied crises at once, such as in 2016 "the Greek debt crisis, Putin's first aggression against Ukraine and the rumblings of Brexit in the background, and the refugee crisis in Syria spilling over into Europe," without them being clearly connected by a "single common denominator" (Tooze, 2023). This "polycrisis" situation has since intensified in our post-Covid, financially destabilised, climate-crisis-ridden and war-torn world, with the 2023 World Economic Forum's *Global Risks Report* describing it as one "where disparate crises interact such that the overall impact far exceeds the sum of each part" (World Economic Forum, *Global Risks Report*, 2023).

Such an overload of crisis experiences can result in anxiety, particularly also in young people (Weber, 2023). Enhancing critical thinking skills can arguably work against the feeling of overwhelm that often accompanies the experience of "polycrisis" as it can assist in observing the situation more objectively and calmly, rather than being consumed by it. As Stephen Brookfield points out, critical thinking skills can help students "identify the assumptions that frame their thinking and actions and to check out how far these assumptions are accurate and valid" (Brookfield, 2015, p. 155). This skill to become aware of one's own belief system and how that can impact on thought and action has become more paramount than ever—especially also now due to the rise of fake news online (D'Ancona, 2017), which seems to have grown in parallel to the "polycrisis."

Critical thinking can also counter-act the current problem of being overly judgemental, and quickly adopting stereotypes and simplistic binary thinking, which is often caused by an over-reliance on the information obtained via pressing one or two buttons on technological devices. It can encourage us to slow down and pay greater attention, take "informed actions" (Brookfield, 2015, p. 155) and look at an issue from "different perspectives" (*ibid.*). Brookfield largely emphasises the benefits for oneself in his elaboration on critical thinking, arguing that if students become more aware of their underlying assumptions and frames, they are "much better placed to act in ways that further [their own] interests" (*ibid.*). However, I would argue that the aspect of taking into account "different perspectives and possibilities" also establishes a reach beyond oneself to an "other," which is the kind of ethical responsibility I would mostly like to focus on in this article. I am hereby drawing on the philosopher Emmanuel Lévinas, who in "Ethics as First Philosophy" promotes an ethics that is centred around encounters with and responsibility to/for the "other" (Lévinas, 1989, pp. 75-87). Rather than emphasising personal subjectivity, Lévinas proposes looking beyond us and those who are immediately around us and resemble us.

If the facet of critical thinking that reaches out to an "other" is considered, it becomes intertwined with ethical responsibility. This combination can, for instance, be achieved via discussions of ethical scenarios that are linked to "real-world problems" (Ribchester & Healey, 2019, p. 101). As Chris Ribchester and Ruth Healey argue, "well-facilitated [ethical] discussions [...] push students to display the critical thinking skills evident at the upper end of Bloom et al.'s cognitive domain (1956) and the 'organisation' and 'characterisation' of values within the affective domain (1964)" (*ibid.*, p. 103). Looking at an issue or piece of work from various viewpoints can help with keeping an open mind towards other perspectives, developing greater compassion with others and thereby also becoming more ethically responsible public citizens and potential leaders. The examples I will discuss in this article focus to a great extent on how to facilitate such discussions, but also include more embodied, performance-based learning processes, which add a dimension of affective closeness to the—at times—more distanced cognitive discussions. Affect is helpful in two main ways: it adds urgency to resolving an issue and it creates a longer-term awareness and (bodily) memory of an event (Shouse, 2005). As Silvan Tomkins writes, affect "amplifies our awareness […] which activates it that we are forced to be concerned, and concerned immediately" (1995, p. 88). Before turning to the two Drama and Theatre Arts case studies, I would, however, first like to explore some of the challenges that can hinder the teaching and learning of critical thinking skills and ethical responsibility today.

## CHALLENGES POSED BY THE GROWING MARKETISATION OF HIGHER EDUCATION

One of the main difficulties in this context is the growing marketisation of higher education in the UK and the US, which is linked to the enormous influence of neoliberal policies since the 1980s (Giroux, 2010). British and American universities in particular are increasingly being run as businesses designed to make profit and to produce specialized workers. As Joyce Canaan and Wesley Shumar make clear, higher education in these countries:

> […] is imagined and structured to at least two neoliberal assumptions: first, that its institutions should compete to sell their services to student 'customers' in an educational marketplace, and second, that these institutions should produce specialized, highly trained workers with high-tech knowledge that will enable the nation and its elite workers to compete 'freely' on a global economic stage. (Canaan & Shumar, 2008, pp. 4-5)

Neoliberalism thus views students as "customers" rather than "explorers" (Fox, 1983) of knowledge. Such a "consumer" perspective arguably encourages stasis and passivity on the part of the students rather than active participation and accountability, which in turn diminishes both critical thinking skills and ethical responsibility. Instead of students becoming active co-creators in their learning process, they increasingly become the recipients of a university "experience," delivered to them on a silver platter as part of living in an overall "experience economy." This "experience economy" is no longer first and foremost centred around tangible goods and services, but focuses on costumers "spend[ing] time enjoying a series of memorable events that a company stages [...] to engage [them] in a personal way" (Pine & Gilmore, 2011, p. 3). It is important to note that such an experience within the "experience economy" need not necessarily be ethically beneficial in order to be seen as engaging or memorable (*ibid.*, p. xxii). Neither does it need to be beneficial to higher education learning itself. Marios Hadjianastasis has rightly pointed out that higher education institutions are now "university experience providers, aspiring to cater to students' social, recreational and, in fact, sustenance needs" (2021, p. 2). Mere short-term enjoyment during one's time at university is thus threatening to replace joyful and lasting educational growth that reaches beyond the university walls.

Furthermore, Neoliberalism sees higher education as a "product" (Brancaleone & O'Brien, 2011) rather than as an opportunity for personal and societal development, and it places the onus mostly on the individual—rather than society as a whole—to make sure students have access to this "product." This neoliberal rationale, in turn, ultimately resulted in the introduction of student tuition fees in the UK in the late 1990s (Brooks and Waters, 2011). Neoliberal thinking in terms of supply and demand and heightened individualism arguably loses sight of both non-utilitarian considerations in regard to higher education and the need for societal cohesion and support, which in turn decreases both the capacity for critical thinking beyond ideas of "employability"/ "future financial gains" and the ability to take ethical concerns—such as the well-being and needs of "others"—into account. For instance, socially disadvantaged groups, such as students from low-income families, can be discouraged to enter higher education due to the presence of tuition fees (Marcucci & Johnstone, 2007). Samuel M. Natale and Caroline Doran point out that "[a]n ethical crisis has emerged within education […] and intervention is urgently needed" (2012, p. 187). The second part of this article will discuss what such interventionist strategies could look like. But I would like to examine another set of challenges first.

## CHALLENGES POSED BY FAST-PACED TECHNOLOGICAL CHANGES

Another difficulty regarding the enhancement of critical thinking skills and ethical responsibility in higher education teaching and learning is the rapidly changing world brought about by increasingly complex technology and wide-spread digitalisation. While technology can be incorporated into higher education in a useful way—e.g. through the flipped classroom, a blended class, or online lectures/seminars—it can also be counter-productive or even disruptive to the learning process, as Henry C. Lucas, for instance, shows. He argues that such a disruption especially occurs if technology-enhanced learning does not include enough discussion time to promote critical thinking skills:

> [D]iscussion […] is designed to help students learn how to think about and solve problems. […]. Society is changing too rapidly and facts are available to anyone with an Internet connection, so simply teaching today's facts does not necessarily prepare students for the future. Students need to learn how to think critically, so they can successfully negotiate opportunities and threats that we cannot envision today. (Lucas, 2016, p. 8)

Lucas here importantly points out that critical thinking skills are not just about solving today's problems, but also look towards the future and the unknown challenges we are yet to encounter. Furthermore, such skills are not just about knowledge, but also about how to *navigate* knowledge. One would need to add to Lucas' analysis here that the facts which the Internet provides need to be treated with great care, especially since the rise of fake news and conspiracy theories online (D'Ancona, 2017). Students need to learn more and more how to check sources before citing them, which is furthermore becoming increasingly difficult due to the sheer amount of data that is available online. This article does not seek to promote a complete techno-pessimism—for instance, an AI tool like ChatGPT could be incorporated into teaching by letting students search for background information to a certain topic. However, the important additional step would then need to be teaching students how to evaluate that information and how to establish their own line of argumentation, rather than letting ChatGPT create an academic argument *for* them.

Another challenge students encounter today is the increasing speed online and on their devices, which encourages quick decision-making rather than the type of slow and careful deliberation that is part of critical thinking and of democratic decision-making processes. Such speed can, for instance, be seen in the rise of so-called "gamification," whereby economic, political and social contexts take on elements of fast-moving (video) games. This wide-spread "reach of games and game design into everyday life" (Walz & Deterding, 2014, p. 3) emerged particularly around 2010-2011 (*ibid.*). According to Ian Bogost, gamification is not so much about drawing on positive and meaningful aspects of games and playfulness, i.e., for example, the careful mastery of a game by overcoming obstacles; instead, it frequently involves the exploitation of consumers (2014, pp. 72; 76). Gamification reduces playing to a fast and "catchy" stimulus-response experience (Bogost, 2011, p. 131)—often for business and marketing purposes. Steffen P. Walz and Sebastian Deterding, for instance, explain that "[i]n marketing, one finds digital loyalty programs and sweepstakes built around 'customer engagement': checking into a store; sharing or liking posts and product pages of brands on social media platforms" (2014, p. 3). If not conducted with a great amount of awareness, quick responses in the form of like/dislike, yes/no can arguably promote a binary and potentially judgemental and divisive way of thinking, rather than a more complex and gracious manner of perceiving the world.

Furthermore, habitual quick decision-making online or via an app does not only affect critical thinking skills, but also has a potentially harmful influence on ethical responsibility for an "other," as it is often done on one's own—that is, without taking another point of view into account. Therefore, it promotes isolation rather than togetherness and community, which can also affect mental health and personal relationships. As Sherry Turkle has pointed out, growing digitalisation has turned us into paradoxical beings: we are increasingly "alone together," which is also the title of her famous 2011 book. This is often due to the modern-day addiction to screens and devices, multi-tasking and a concomitant lack of attention and time for each other. Our networked life allows us to hide from each other, even as we are seemingly connected to each other: "The world is now full of [...] people who take comfort in being in touch with a lot of people whom they also keep at bay" (Turkle, 2011, p. xlvi).

This act of hiding from each other can also lead to a lack of compassion with another's predicament. As Charles R. Chaffin makes clear, while the internet presents us with compassion-evoking "images and discussions of suffering and upheaval" (Chaffin, 2023), it does so in such quantity and frequency that this "overload" can lead to compassion fatigue, which he defines as "a state of emotional and physical exhaustion from repeated exposure to some element of human need" (*ibid.*). It is a term that is usually associated with "first responders, therapists, and healthcare workers in regular contact with people dealing with extraordinarily difficult periods" (*ibid.*), but Chaffin applies it to the effects of over-exposure to suffering online, arguing that especially the graphic nature of the seemingly limitless number of images and videos of victims disseminated online result in a feeling of numbness towards other people's fates and can lead to inaction on behalf of others.

In order to counter some of the detrimental effects a growing reliance on technology can have on both critical thinking and ethical responsibility, one would need to employ pedagogies that ideally help the students focus their attention and engage in meaningful ways in group discussions and reflective learning processes. Such pedagogies would support the students in becoming co-creators and explorers of their own learning processes and would look less towards quick decision-making and short-termism and more towards longer-term thinking and sustainability. They would take into account the well-being of others, e.g. also through considering "real-life" effects/scenarios based on the tasks presented to them and the discussions in class. While this list and the following examples are in no way meant to be exhaustive, I would now like to discuss two case studies from my own field of Drama and Theatre Arts to demonstrate how some of the above-mentioned goals could be achieved through a use of pedagogies of critical distancing and affective closeness. The examples chosen here from this field can effectively highlight the usefulness of this two-pronged approach through their own combination of artistic nearness to "real-life" socio-political issues as well as their artistic distancing.

In an era of "post-truth politics" (D'Ancona, 2017, p. 20), which is marked by "the triumph of the visceral over the rational, the deceptively simple over the honestly complex" (*ibid.*), it might seem useful to *solely* emphasise rationality and critical distancing. However, as will be demonstrated here, it is vital to bring together both pedagogies of critical distancing and affective closeness to enhance both critical thinking skills and ethical responsibility. Distancing strategies can work against a sense of overwhelm in times of "polycrisis," and techniques of closeness can prevent numbness, "compassion fatigue" as well as inaction in this turbulent age. While, overall, critical thinking skills appear to be more readily linked to distancing techniques, and the enhancement of ethical responsibility seems more aligned with the strategies of closeness, it will be shown that interlinking both pedagogies helps to promote both skill/value sets—critical thinking skills and ethical responsibility—at the same time.

## CASE STUDY 1: AN AFFECTIVE ENCOUNTER AND CRITICAL ENGAGEMENT WITH THE EMOTION OF ANGER IN THEATRE AND PHILOSOPHY IN TIMES OF ONLINE "OUTRAGE"

To create a more immediate and affective encounter with the largely abstract, and seemingly distant, concept of anger as it seems to appear in philosophy, I first let the students affectively recall instances of online and "real-life" outrage—where they either encountered easily enraged individuals or they themselves potentially felt angered by a certain situation or comment. They did not need to share the exact details, but I asked them to remember and, if possible, to express either verbally or non-verbally, what it felt like on a more visceral level. As Melissa Gregg and Gregory J. Seigworth make clear, "affect is found in those intensities that pass body to body [...], in those resonances that circulate about, between, and sometimes stick to bodies and worlds" (2010, p. 1). This transmission of intensities can result in a visceral reaction—and a "drive [...] toward movement" and "thought" (*ibid.*). Affect thus involves both visceral experience and thought. The affective experience is in itself neither ethically good nor bad, but it can help "move" the students towards greater compassion and ethical responsibility via a body-to-body transmission, e.g. of feelings of hurt as a consequence of being faced with online outrage. I then established a more cognitive and critical connection to Seneca's stoic philosophy, which, for example, draws attention to the destructive results of anger in *De Ira* (On Anger). In light of his "real-life" experiences with the Roman emperor Nero's anger, Seneca argued that the passionate state of being enraged leads to volatility and the inability to control one's actions (*De Ira* 1.7; 2.3-4). I then discussed with the students in how far their experiences of online outrage would perhaps speak to/not speak to Seneca's ideas.

As a drama example I used a so-called Revenge Tragedy—in this case Seneca's play *Thyestes*—for this topic, as emotions like anger often drive revenge. The genre was a popular one especially for the stage from "fifth-century Athens, with its Orestes and Electra plays, its *Hecuba* and *Medea*; the Rome of Seneca's *Thyestes*; seventeenth-century Spain, notable for tragedies of honour; the France of Corneille and Racine; the England of Kyd, Shakespeare, and Marston" (Kerrigan 1997, p. 3). John Kerrigan explains the popularity of the link between revenge and drama as follows:

> Vengeance offers the writer a compelling mix of ingredients: strong situations shaped by violence; ethical issues for debate; a volatile, emotive mixture of loss and agitated grievance. The avenger, isolated and vulnerable, can achieve heroic grandeur by coming to personify nemesis. No less dramatically, groups of characters fuse in vindictive conspiracy through lurid ritual and oath-taking, discovering between themselves a sympathy which can exalt those forms of relationship—such as hold, for instance, between kin—which given cultures find it useful to celebrate. (Kerrigan, 1997, p. 3)

*Thyestes*, a first-century (CE) Roman tragedy, tells the story of two brothers, Atreus and Thyestes, who engage in a bitter struggle for the control of the kingdom of their deceased father Pelops. Act I shows how a Fury from the underworld, one of the Erinyes, drives their battle on, but it is also the brothers' own decisions and enmity that continue a seemingly never-ending cycle of anger and revenge. As Thyestes had seduced Atreus' wife before the start of the play, the action now mainly focuses on Atreus' revenge. He orders the killing of Thyestes' three sons and has them served up to his brother in a horrible feast. The play ends with Atreus revealing to Thyestes that he has been fed his own children, but instead of offering a sense of Atreus having come up victorious, the play indicates that this is a destructive cycle which will most likely continue. There is arguably no sense of closure at the end.

There has been a long discussion in regard to how closely Seneca's plays reflect his own stoic philosophy. Seneca's own emphasis on the volatility caused by anger—and the promotion of *constantia* (steadfastness) and *ratio* (reason) instead—seems to stand in contrast to the angry Atreus' seemingly calm use of *ratio* in plotting his revenge. As Atreus does not seem overcome by passionate emotion, this contrast has been used to demonstrate a kind of (mis)application of Stoicism for vicious and selfish ends in Seneca's play. In his article "Commanding Constantia in Senecan Tragedy," Christopher Star therefore speaks about a "use of Stoicism to achieve unstoic goals" (2006, p. 210) in this context. Nevertheless, the role of (the) Fury, who is seen as underpinning the play, arguably depicts how previous anger can drive such a misuse of reason and Stoicism. Atreus had some time to carefully plot his revenge after being enraged by the seduction of his wife by his own brother. While the harmful results of anger are perhaps not immediate, they are clearly present.

During the two sessions we spent on this topic, I asked the students to contrast Seneca's view on the destructiveness of anger with the—self-defined—black Lesbian poet and philosopher Audre Lorde's much more positive perspective on anger. Lorde spoke on this topic in her keynote address at the annual conference of the National Women's Studies Association in 1981. In the address, she argues against fearing anger, and fully embraces this emotion instead. She states that speaking up in anger in response to instances of injustice such as racism does not mean that one would kill someone. Killing and a destructive kind of fury comes from self-centred hatred, not anger itself: "Hatred is the fury of those who do not share our goals, and its object is death and destruction. Anger is the grief of distortions between peers, and its object is change" (Lorde, 1981, p. 8). She describes the necessity to openly express "the anger of exclusion, of unquestioned privilege, or racial distortions, of silence, ill-use, stereotyping, defensiveness, mis-naming, betrayal, and co-opting" (*ibid*.), especially in the face of the expectation typically imposed on women, particularly women of colour, not to voice any critique of the patriarchy or other unjust, oppressive systems—either at all or not "too harshly" (*ibid*., p. 7). However, she says, such silence due to "unexpressed anger" (*ibid.*, p. 8) would lead to "changelessness" (*ibid.*, p. 9). In order to bring about social and political change, one needs to find a way to "translate[…]" (*ibid.*, p. 8) anger into effective tools "to examine and to alter all the repressive conditions of our lives" (*ibid.*). This also means turning away from any kind of self-centredness and finding allies in other "women, people of color, Lesbians, gay men, poor people" (*ibid.*) via listening closely to their anger in order to discover "mutual empowerment" (*ibid.*, p. 10). Listening, in turn, implies looking behind the "presentation" (*ibid.*, p. 9) of anger and delving into the "substance" (ibid.) behind it. Thus, according to Lorde, if anger is used constructively and not in a self-centred way, it can combat various forms of oppression as it can lead to insight (*ibid.*), growth (*ibid.*, p. 7) and change (*ibid.*, p. 8).

The exercise of comparing the two views on "anger"—the Senecan and the Lordean one—can enhance both critical thinking skills and ethical responsibility. When the students were asked to discuss the two views of anger, as well as the play *Thyestes* and secondary sources such as Christopher Star's above-cited article, they found some common ground between Lorde's definition of hatred and the destructive anger that Seneca speaks about. They also saw how modern Internet outrage often falls within the more self-centred, destructive kind, rather than the constructive use of anger that Lorde speaks about. The students realised that it takes time to closely analyse the two philosophical texts, since both views—Seneca's and Lorde's—include a complexity and nuances that could be easily missed, if they were not discussed in depth. For instance, while Seneca does not mention a usefulness of anger, he shows in his play *Thyestes* that a seemingly virtuous quality (*ratio*) can be misused for vengeful purposes if it becomes self-centred and destructive. Lorde, on the other hand, detects that anger can be harnessed in a constructive way, but also includes the caveat that self-centredness prevents the usefulness of anger and turns it into destructive hatred.

Detecting such complexity and nuance regarding understandings of "anger" can be particularly helpful in this day and age of quick judgement and divisiveness online. Dealing with potentially hard to read philosophy in particular can arguably further critical thinking as well as ethical responsibility—e.g. in the face of instances of injustice. It can be seen as what David Perkins has described as a "troublesome" type of learning and knowledge (1999, p. 10), i.e. it can be "complex, with many pieces of information" (*ibid.*). One might need to overcome a certain initial obstacle in order to acquire a transformed way of thinking. This is why, building on Perkins' ideas, Jan Meyer and Ray Land have developed the notion of "threshold concepts," i.e. "conceptual gateways" or "portals" which "lead to a previously inaccessible, and initially perhaps 'troublesome', way of thinking about something" (2005, p. 373). "Anger" can be regarded as such a "threshold concept," and for topics such as this one, it is vital that the students engage carefully with texts and performances, as well as with their own affective experiences of anger and outrage. This helps them look beyond the "surface level," and to be able to be patient, alert and capable of analysing difficult passages or scenes in greater depth. Instead of "surface learning" (Race, 2007, p. 36), which might be akin to what numerous Internet sources offer, students can here become fully engaged in deep learning.

## CASE STUDY 2: GREEN STUDIES, DISCUSSIONS AND EMBODIED AFFECTIVE ENCOUNTERS IN THE FACE OF THE CURRENT CLIMATE CRISIS

To demonstrate another variation in the interlinking of the two pedagogies, the second case study brings together discussions with a more actively *embodied* encounter than before, as the students involved performed various scenes as part of a first-year practical module called "Engaging Performance." I connected these exercises to the topic of climate change and Green Studies, and aimed to intertwine critically distanced discussions with embodied affective encounters in order to both work against overwhelming "climate anxiety" and promote active compassion at the same time.

Green Studies has various definitions, but a wider one is that it comprises "the study of the relationship of the human and the non-human" (Garrard, 2004, p. 5). The main issue that is often identified in this relationship is the fact that humans have traditionally seen themselves as being "above" animals and the natural world, which has led to an increasing exploitation of the planet and a destruction of large amounts of animal species. In order to counteract this arguably harmful binary opposition and hierarchy of humans vs. animals and the natural world, one would have to create exercises that destabilise such an opposition and work against an all-knowing, domineering human gaze.

Enhancing Critical Thinking Skills and Ethical Responsibility

In the context of my first-year practical Drama and Theatre Arts module "Engaging Performance," which uses mostly non-verbal, physical theatre to address wider national and global crises, but also employs textual passages to some extent, I developed the following exercises that aimed to enhance critical thinking skills regarding the relationship between humans and animals—as well as promote ethical responsibility towards the animals as a kind of Lévinasian "other."

- First, I asked the students to think of—and enact—stereotypical animal movements.
- Then I encouraged them to reflect on what might have been problematic about these portrayals in light of Green Studies—e.g., I asked the question: did the first exercise lead to some uncomfortable feelings, and if so, why?
- Next, I let the students bring to mind favourite animals or pets, and asked them—how could we do these pets greater justice in performance? And how could we extend such a more complex/compassionate portrayal to other animals? We collected various answers.
- Then I showed them an example in which animals were shrouded in mystery, which can create a sense of awe in the audience and thereby work against an all-knowing, domineering human gaze.
- Finally, I let the students experiment and create more empowering portrayals of animals—especially by focusing on evoking mystery, e.g. by using awe-inspiring music and movement sequences or portraying encounters between humans and nature/animals where the humans' all-knowing gaze/sense of dominance seemed to fail. However, I also allowed space for their own approaches.

The example I focused on with the students as part of this set of exercises was Deke Weaver's *Unreliable Bestiary* (2009-ongoing), which is a long-term theatre project involving climate change. Weaver wants to create a performance for every letter of the alphabet, each letter representing an endangered species or threatened habitat. The *Bestiary* started with the production of *Monkey* in 2009, followed by *Elephant* (2010), *Wolf* (2013), *Bear* (2016-17), *Tiger* (2019) and *Cetacean (The Whale)* (2023). This is an excerpt from *Elephant*:

Is it true that elephants are completely silent when they walk?

Yes. It is true.

Is it true that elephants have seven sets of teeth?

Yes. It is true.

Is it true that elephants are herded by infernal gods, wandering the frozen blackness of the underworld?

Yes. It is true.

'The blood of the elephant, it is said, is remarkably cold, for which reason, in the parching heats of summer, it is sought by the dragon with remarkable avidity [...]' (Pliny the Elder). (Weaver, 2014, p. 141)

In this performance piece, Weaver brings together a presentation of scientific facts regarding the specific species and habitat, on the one hand, with unreliable narration and the tradition of the medieval bestiary, on the other. This establishes a combination of fact and fiction, anatomy and imagination. The pre-modern bestiary in itself already establishes a link between an interest in proto-science with an almost magical depiction of animals. As Una Chaudhuri and Joshua Williams have pointed out regarding Weaver's work, this "more-than-scientific" perspective on the "relation to other animals" (2020, p. 72) is apt nowadays as "the Anthropocene has plunged us into a post-scientific—or at least deeply science-sceptical—time [...]. As climate change accelerates, it topples the very scientific models and predictive systems through which we have been attempting to apprehend it" (*ibid.*, pp. 74-75). Nature in a way eludes human models of trying to understand it.

As Weaver himself makes clear, his performances work with the affect of "wonder"—yet not in the sense of a sensationalist type of wonder, but more in terms of a "plain old wonder" (qtd. in Chaudhuri & Williams, 2020, p. 80), a mundane understanding of awe. Rather than aiming for short-term spectacular effects, Weaver is interested in art that "can have tremendous long-term effects if it burrows into somebody's imagination, like a seed growing into an oak tree," and hopes that "maybe some of [his] work will sink into one or more people who might carry the idea somewhere else" (Weaver & Lux, 2012, pp. 36-37). While he does seem to realise that we need to act *now* in the face of harmful climate change, he also wants to cultivate a more longer-term outlook on nature, animals and the climate. Interestingly, he thereby works against current short-termism, which is also often the cause of climate change. Weaver is aiming for mystery and depth—rather than superficial knowledge.

Recent research into the affect of "awe," defined as "the feeling of being in the presence of something vast that transcends your current understanding of the world" (Keltner, 2023a, p. 7) shows that especially the type of wonder that can emerge out of seemingly mundane situations can have a very powerful effect. As opposed to ideas put forward in connection to the 18th-century "sublime," Dacher Keltner points out that awe does not need to take the form of a spectacular encounter with a vast landscape like the Grand Canyon or the Alps—which not everyone might have access to and can therefore seem elitist in this day and age. He writes: "The cultivation of awe can be done, as with mindfulness practices, anywhere, and only takes a minute or two" (Keltner, 2023b). Awe "is always around you, if you just take a moment to pause and open your mind to what is vast and mysterious nearby" (*ibid.*). This experience can have a positive effect on the relationship between different people as well as between humans and the non-human: "people recently exposed to awe are kinder, more environmentally friendly, and better connected to others" (*ibid.*). Through its power of connection, awe is able to "respond[...] to the crises of individualism, of excessive self-focus, loneliness, and the cynicism of our times" (*ibid.*). The both scientific and beyond-scientific view presented by Weaver's work—together with its focus on awe—arguably shifts power away from a human all-knowing gaze and entices curiosity about, and compassion with, the animals. It works with critical thinking and scientific facts, but also evokes ethical responsibility towards an "other"—in this case endangered species and habitats. This is why it lends itself very well to the teaching of the skills emphasised in this article—via pedagogies of both critical distancing and affective closeness.

## CONCLUSION

Using two examples from the field of Drama and Theatre Arts—Seneca's *Thyestes* and Deke Weaver's *Unreliable Bestiary*—which in themselves can be seen as displaying elements of both nearness and distance in their artistic responses to "real-life" socio-political issues—I developed an approach that interlinks pedagogies of critical distancing and affective closeness to enhance both critical thinking and ethical responsibility. This was done in order to show how "graduate attributes" such as the two skill/value sets that I focused on can indeed become fully reflected by the curriculum and the pedagogies, rather than remaining superficial and potentially tokenistic. Each case study involved slightly different aspects regarding the interlinking of the two pedagogies, as I emphasised text-based discussions and active student performance, in turn. The subject of Drama and Theatre Arts particularly lends itself to this kind of pedagogical blend—as plays/performances themselves can work both on a critical and affective level in an engaged encounter with the audience/students. However, the two-pronged approach of employing pedagogies of critical distancing and affective closeness in UK higher education could also be used in other literary and artistic subjects, as well as in the social sciences. It can be achieved through emphasising both theoretical analysis and an affective connection to a topic that is linked to socio-political issues. In scientific subjects it could be reached through a similar approach that the *Unreliable Bestiary* uses—e.g. by pointing out what knowledge can be attained through science and where perhaps the (mysterious) limits lie that forces such as nature still impose on us. The two-pronged approach of critical distancing and affective closeness can create a kind of slowing down, humbleness, and connection, which in this day and age of seemingly quick individual mastery, driven by both the increasing marketisation of higher education and the fast pace of technological change, can promote a deeper understanding as well as a greater compassion with a subject/a Lévinasian "other" at hand.

**SUGGESTED CITATION**

Redling, E. (2024). Enhancing critical thinking skills and ethical responsibility in UK higher education in times of "polycrisis": Two case studies from drama and theatre arts. *ArtsPraxis, 11* (1), pp. 83-105.

**REFERENCES**

Bauman, Z. (2000). *Liquid modernity*. Cambridge, MA: Polity Press.

Beck, U. (1992). *Risk society: Towards a new modernity*. London: Sage.

Bogost, I. (2011). *How to do things with videogames*. Minneapolis, MN: University of Minnesota Press.

Bogost, I. (2014). Why gamification is bullshit. In S. P. Walz & S. Deterding (Eds.), *The gameful world: Approaches, issues, applications,* pp. 65-79, Cambridge, MA: MIT Press.

Brancaleone, D. & O'Brien, S. (2011). Educational commodification and the (economic) sign value of learning outcomes, *British Journal of Sociology of Education*, *32* (4), pp. 501-519.

Brookfield, S. (2015). *The skillful teacher: On technique, trust, and responsiveness in the classroom*. San Francisco, CA: Jossey-Bass.

Brooks, R. & Waters, J. (2011). Fees, funding and overseas study: mobile UK students and educational inequalities. *Sociological Research Online*, *16* (2), pp. 19-28.

Canaan, J. E. & Shumar, W. (2008). Higher Education in the Era of Globalization and Neoliberalism. In J. E. Canaan & W. Shumar (Eds.), *Structure and agency in the neoliberal university,* pp. 1-30. New York: Routledge.

Chaffin, C. R. (2023). How to keep our compassion when it's needed most. *Psychology Today*.

Chaudhuri, U. & Williams, J. (2020). The play at the end of world: Deke Weaver's unreliable bestiary and the theatre of extinction. In K. Shepherd-Barr (Ed.), *The Cambridge companion to theatre and science,* pp. 70-84. Cambridge: Cambridge University Press.

Cribb, A. & Gewirtz, S. (2013). The hollowed-out university? A critical analysis of changing institutional and academic norms in UK higher education. *Discourse: Studies in the Cultural Politics of*

*Education*, 34, pp. 338-350.

Cusack, C. (2013). Introduction. In L. Nevitt, *Theatre and violence,* pp. ix-xii. Basingstoke: Palgrave Macmillan.

D'Ancona, M. (2017). *Post truth: The new war on truth and how to fight back*. London: Ebury Press.

Fox, D. (1983). Personal theories of teaching. *Studies in Higher Education*, 8 (2), pp. 151-163.

Garrard, G. (2004). *Ecocriticism*. London: Routledge.

Giroux, H. A. (2010). Bare pedagogy and the scourge of neoliberalism: Rethinking higher education as a democratic public sphere. *The Educational Forum*, 74, pp. 184-196.

Gregg, M. & Seigworth, G. J. (2010). An inventory of shimmers. In M. Gregg & G. J. Seigworth (Eds.), *The affect theory reader,* pp. 1-26. Durham, NC: Duke University Press.

Hadjianastasis, M. (2021). Higher education as a product: A concept tested during pandemic times. *Educational Developments*, 22 (3), pp.1-5.

Hill, J., Walkington, H. & France, D. (2016). Graduate attributes: implications for higher education practice and policy. *Journal of Geography in Higher Education*, 40 (2), pp. 155-163.

Keltner, D. (2023a). *Awe: The Transformative Power of Everyday Wonder*. London: Allen Lane.

Keltner, D. (2023b). Here's why you need to be cultivating awe in your life. *The Guardian*.

Kerrigan, J. (1997). *Revenge Tragedy: Aeschylus to Armageddon*. Oxford: Clarendon Press.

Lévinas, E. (1989). *The Lévinas reader*, ed. Séan Hand. London: Blackwell.

Lorde, Audre (1981). The uses of anger. *Women's Studies Quarterly*, 9 (3), pp. 7-10.

Lucas, H. C. (2016). *Technology and the disruption of higher education*. Hackensack, NJ: World Scientific.

Marcucci, P. N. & Johnstone, D. B. (2007). Tuition fee policies in a comparative perspective: Theoretical and political rationales. *Journal of Higher Education Policy and Management*, 29 (1), pp. 25-40.

Meyer, J. H. F. & Land, R. (2005). Threshold concepts and troublesome knowledge (2): Epistemological considerations and a conceptual framework for teaching and learning. *Higher*

*Education, 49*, pp. 373-388.

Natale, S. M. & Doran, C. (2012). Marketization of education: An ethical dilemma. *Journal of Business Ethics, 105* (2), pp. 187-196.

Nevitt, L. (2013). *Theatre and violence*. Basingstoke: Palgrave Macmillan.

Perkins, D. (1999). The many faces of constructivism. *Educational Leadership, 57* (3), pp. 6-11.

Pine, B. J. II & Gilmore, J. H. (2011). *The experience economy*. Boston, MA: Harvard Business School Press.

Race, P. (2007). *The lecturer's toolkit: A resource for developing assessment, learning and teaching*. London: Routledge.

Ribchester, C. & Healey, R. L. (2019). Realism, reflection and responsibility: The challenge of writing effective scenarios to support the development of ethical thinking skills. *Journal of Further and Higher Education, 43* (1), pp. 101-114.

Seneca, L. A. (1928). *Moral Essays: Vol. 1: De providentia, de constantia, de ira, de clementia*. Cambridge, MA: Harvard University Press.

Shouse, E. (2005). Feeling, emotion, affect. *M/C Journal, 8* (6).

Star, C. (2006). Commanding constantia in Senecan tragedy. *Transactions of the American Philological Association, 136* (1), pp. 207-244.

Stehr, N. (2001). *The fragility of modern societies: Knowledge and risk in the information age*. London: Sage.

Tomkins, S. (1995). *Exploring affect: The selected writings of Silvan S. Tomkins*. Ed. E.V. Demos. Cambridge: Cambridge University Press.

Tooze, A. (2023). Can the word "polycrisis" help us make sense of the post-COVID world? Historian Adam Tooze has his say. Interview with H. Park (Radio Davos). Published online: February 2023.

Turkle, S. (2011). *Alone together: Why we expect more from technology and less from each other*. New York: Basic Books.

Universities UK. (2024). Letter to the Prime Minister.

Walz, S. P. & Deterding, S. (2014). An introduction to the gameful world. In S. P. Walz & S. Deterding (Eds.), *The gameful world: Approaches, issues, applications,* pp. 1-13. Cambridge, MA: MIT Press.

Weaver, D. (2014). Excerpts from *Elephant*. In U. Chaudhuri & H.

Hughes (Eds.), *Animal acts: Performing species today*, pp. 140-161. Ann Arbor, MI: The University of Michigan Press.

Weaver, D. & Lux, M. (2012). The unreliable bestiary. *Antennae: The Journal of Nature in Visual Culture*, 22, pp. 31-40.

Weber, A. M. (2023). *Generation Krise Hoffnung: Wie junge Menschen zwischen Klimawandel, Krieg und Selfie-Sucht die Zukunft gestalten*. Essen: Klartext Verlag.

Williams, Z. (2024). The Goldsmiths crisis: How cuts and culture wars sent Universities into a death spiral. *The Guardian*.

World Economic Forum (2023). *Global Risks Report*.


## AUTHOR BIOGRAPHY

Ellen Redling is a lecturer in Drama and Theatre Arts, University of Birmingham, UK. She has written numerous articles on contemporary theatre and performance, and co-edited a volume on *Non-standard Forms of Contemporary Drama and Theatre* (Trier: WVT, 2008). She has also published books on Victorian Literature (*Allegorical Thackeray*, Zurich: LIT, 2015, which looked at intersections between allegorical plays and Victorian novels) and on the Gothic (*Gothic Transgressions*, co-edited with Christian Schneider, Zurich: LIT, 2015). She is currently working on a new monograph project: *Theatres of Disruption in 21st-Century Britain: Political Plays and Performances in Turbulent Times* (under contract with Bloomsbury).

# Social Justice and Fringe Theatre in Higher Education

**DERMOT DALY**

LEEDS CONSERVATOIRE AND LEEDS BECKETT UNIVERSITY

## ABSTRACT

Theatre and performance have long been used to platform, challenge, and agitate for social justice. Using contemporary work focussed on marginalised communities can facilitate and broaden the reach and understanding of such work. This paper reports on a case study using It's A MotherF\*\*King Pleasure (FlawBored, 2023) in a formal higher education setting, examining what can be gained in the use(s) of such work. In moving through arguments advocating for working with 'fringe' artists and their work, the benefits of conscious enaction of critical pedagogy and the highlighting of the potential benefits to students—and educators—in their understanding of social justice, this paper argues for the inclusion of those new artists making work now, into the teaching material. The case study emphasises the importance and ability of creating a space in higher education (and beyond) for open and engaged inquiry into deeply held viewpoints, with suggestions of how to enact it, offered.

Social justice, and the use of theatre to promote, challenge and understand it have a long history, from Lorraine Hansberry's *A Raisin in the Sun* (first performed in 1959), Martin Sherman's *Bent* (1979) and Caryl Churchill's *Top Girls* (1982) through to *It's A MotherF\*\*King Pleasure (2023)* by FlawBored—the textual focus of the case study discussed in this paper. Respectively, these pieces challenge—and are thematically engaged with—racism, homophobia, sexism and ableism. These, unfortunately perennial ills, *can* be addressed in the curricula and teaching materials that students may be introduced to at both under- and post-graduate study, but the study of theatre and its use for the advancement and understanding of social justice is not uniform across performance-based courses in higher education. Thematic focus on race, sexuality, gender and ableism are not routinely offered in, and on, the canons used and/or referred to.

Hansberry, Sherman and Churchill's work can be argued to be part of the canon of work which is understood to contain works that are 'authoritative in our culture' (Bloom, 1994, p. 2). The scholarly study that has been dedicated to these pieces (for example—see Rose, 2014; Sterling, 2002; Cameron, 2009) and their places of debut[1] can be seen as validation of this assertion. Their ever-topical ideas can be addressed against the context in which they were written, and contrasted or juxtaposed by the context in which they are received/offered. Pieces like Flawbored's, by virtue of its 'newness', can only be viewed in a contemporary context; the same context and temporality in which current students are learning and working.

In working with new(er) fringe artists, and their texts and ideas, access is created for students and lecturers to engage with the new trends and emergent themes that are leading to the exciting and multifaceted provocations which are informing contemporary theatre and performance. The ability for social change, and the tools to facilitate it, are embedded in critical pedagogy and through that

---

[1] *A Raisin in the Sun* was first performed at the Ethel Barrymore Theatre on Broadway with *Bent* and *Top Girls* both at The Royal Court in London. *It's A MotherF\*\*King Pleasure* debuted at VAULT festival – a fringe theatre festival in south-east London

pedagogical understanding the skills and desire to create the work that will lead to that change can be gained. Freire remarks that '[l]iberating education consists in acts of cognition, not transferrals of information' (Freire, 2000, p. 79), and the making of theatre, it can be argued, is a pure act of cognition which results in transferal of information. In understanding that '[t]heatre is a form of knowledge, [which] should and *can also be* the means of transforming society' (Boal, 2002, p. 16, emphasis added) it can be argued that those studying theatre, once empowered to see the changes needed, can use their acquired skill and resident fervour, to change the world. The possibility, therefore, to include 'fringe' artists and their work in higher education study, and therefore understanding, is an excitingly potent prospect for all concerned. Keeping the field up to date by being actively engaged in what is happening now, contextualised by what has gone before, is an immeasurably important facet of the work that socially engaged theatre and theatre makers should be immersing themselves in. Looking to the statistics that delineate the age profile[2] of those lecturing, teaching and therefore choosing texts, it can be deduced that the education, worldview and base knowledge of those choosing the plays are, at best, often in the *near*-contemporary[3]; exploration of the riches that fringe theatre can offer can act to address this.

If that exploration is not possible due to factors including geography, there are a growing number of initiatives to remedy the gaps in knowledge should they exist. Projects such as Lit in Colour explicitly addresses 'how literature is experienced by students from the age of seven in primary school, until the end of sixth form or college' (*Lit in Colour | Penguin Random House*, 2023); Multiplay Drama commissions 'established writers and distinctive new voices' to create 'large-cast plays, specifically written to be performed by and appeal to young people' which 'span a wide range of styles, setting and subject matter' (*What Is Multiplay Drama? | Multiplay Drama*, n.d.) and 1623 Theatre company's Queer Folio in which '60 queer artists joined members of the LGBTQ+ community to co-create […] new shows […]

---

[2] Using the 2022/23 Higher Education Statistics Agency (HESA) collected data on academic staff across higher education we can see that 29% of all academic staff are between the ages of 36-45; with 25% between 26-35 and 23% between 46-55. (*Who's Working in HE?: Personal Characteristics | HESA*, 2024).

[3] 72% of all academic staff would have completed their undergraduate education *at least* 15 years prior (*Who's Working in HE?: Personal Characteristics | HESA*, 2024)

inspired by Shakespeare's First Folio and queer experiences today' (*Queer Folio—1623 Theatre Company*, n.d.) are alternate sources of texts should engagement in, and with, fringe theatre be difficult. To build for a new world of broader and more nuanced representation, the present needs to be understood outside of the structures that have been held sacrosanct. The only way to create change is to change. The contemporary world is the one into which students will emerge at the completion of their studies and it is the understanding of where we are—both metaphorically and philosophically—that will influence where we could be.

FlawBored's *It's A MotherF\*\*King Pleasure* was first performed at VAULT festival at the beginning of 2023 with a run at the Edinburgh Fringe Festival following in the summer of that year. It has oft been noted that the 'Edinburgh Festival Fringe has proved to be an important incubator for theatre and comedy shows that end up on the West End, Off-Broadway, and even Broadway' (Putnam, 2023), indeed *It's A MotherF\*\*King Pleasure* found itself in an Off-Broadway theatre toward the beginning of 2024[4]. In understanding that the relationship between fringe and, capitalistically minded, commercial theatre is 'deeply entwined and interdependent [...] with producers working across both, and artists flitting between one and the other' (Gardner, 2021) it must be acknowledged that the work found in fringe contexts can be used to teach the art and artistry of theatremaking, unsullied or diluted by the commercial need to make money. Art, freed from the need to make money, is often more in touch with the emergent trends and concerns that socially engaged theatre is rooted in.

## FLAWBORED: IT'S A MOTHERF\*\*KING PLEASURE

FlawBored are a disability led theatre company. Formed in 2021 by Samuel Brewer, Aarian Mehrabani and Chloe Palmer, they aim to 'create meta theatrical work with dark irreverence [aiming] to address complex and uncomfortable issues surrounding identity which no one has the answers to' (*FlawBored | Home*, n.d.). *It's A MotherF\*\*King Pleasure* addresses these issues head on.

The main narrative of the piece explores the monetisation of disability—the creation and exploitation of 'able anxiety'. Blind talent

---

[4] The show played a two and a half week run at SoHo Playhouse in January 2024.

manager Tim, alongside blind influencer Ross and their anxious HR manager Helen, set out on this mission, eventually realising that their manipulation of peoples' desire to fit in, leads to unintended and tragic consequences. In a parallel story 'Aarian', 'Sam' and 'Chloe' (somewhat grotesque versions of the actors playing them) are aiming to deliver a fully accessible show but consistently run into complications, frustrating and making plain the difficulties and hypocrisies that are often seen in the making of 'fully' accessible theatre.

All three founder members graduated from the Royal Central School of Speech and Drama (CSSD) in 2020. Two of the company—Samuel and Aarian—are registered blind and are male identifying, Chloe, the third member, is female identifying. After graduating, Samuel became a co-director of The Diversity Initiative which had the stated aim of addressing 'under-representation, access and diversity in UK drama schools' (Rodgers, 2022, p. 2); Aarian, in 2020, took part in The RXConnect Panel Event: *House Of Bernarda Alba* (rxtheatre, 2020) centred around the Graeae[5] show of the same name, and hosted by the Manchester Royal Exchange Theatre. The panel discussed issues around the Covid-19 lockdowns in the UK and how disabled people were disproportionately affected, moving to imagining a future where theatre makes even more space for the same people. Chloe has worked, as an actor, almost exclusively on new work which has been written and/or directed by people who are marginalised. These details are important as they suggest an impetus and context for the work that the founders aim to do in, and with, FlawBored. These perspectives and beliefs are formative in their view of the world and the way the world views them. It is precisely because of these experiences and viewpoints that their work was judged to be exemplary for a project rooted in social justice with an angle toward societal change.

---

[5] 'Graeae is founded on the mission to create theatrical excellence through the vision and practice of Deaf, disabled, and neurodiverse artists. The experiences of these artists are part of Graeae's genesis, the early productions devised by the company were specifically written to combat societal expectations of disabled people. Over time, the company has produced original works, cabarets, Shakespeare, musicals, and everything in between. While not every show specifically speaks to the Deaf, disabled, and neurodivergent experience, they are all inherently Graeae.'

## THE PROJECT: AIMS AND OBJECTIVES

The project was run as part of a module called 'Pilot Project', which is a 20 credit, core—and therefore compulsory—module taught in semester one at level 6 of the BA (Hons.) Theatre and Performance course at Leeds Beckett University. It has the express aim of facilitating collaboration between the students and an artist in the creation of 'an innovative and sophisticated performance product' (Leeds Beckett University, 2022)—the final product is often performed to level 4 and 5 students as well as faculty staff. Importantly, this is not a public performance opportunity, taking away a perceived pressure of it having to be 'perfect' in order to attract an agent; the emphasis is placed on the opportunity for learning.

Given that this is a project in the final year of the three-year undergraduate degree, there is a clear drive to prepare students for the world outside of the institution. There is a recognition that '[h]uman activity is theory and practice; it is reflection and action' (Freire, 2000, p. 125), and if we are to see their previous two years as theory heavy, this year—and module in particular—is most certainly practice.

The introduction of the 'new' into this teaching space allows the new—in this case FlawBored—to begin to lay claim to authoritatively articulating ideas, themes and practice in 'our' culture that is ripe for study and scholarly understanding. In doing so, however, there must be a consideration of the ethics and broader ramifications of such an introduction—there is a tautological contention that just as all work that can be studied should be studied, not all work that should be studied is. A positive two-way learning journey could be enacted if those who are to be studied are informed and involved. When extant new work is not used for public performance, it is often used without the full knowledge of the originators. This precludes theatre makers from knowing and understanding the far-reaching effects of the work that they make whilst also not facilitating a level of ethical working and care. This is important. There must be constant and consistent communication between the educational and professional space, else each will exist in a silo of its own making and not make the gains that are clearly there to be had. Doing so on this project allowed it to be known to FlawBored that they were not to be positioned as a proxy for *all* disability led work but as an example of *one* specific way of creating disability led work. It allowed the project to involve them, as theatre makers *and* individuals.

**THE PROJECT: FIRST STEPS**

Students were able to contextualise their understanding of the piece through direct contact with the theatremakers—an ability for the training world to talk, directly, to the professional world. Via email they asked:

- What influenced you to make the play?
- What reaction have you had?
- What reaction did you hope to have?
- Why is it important that those 'on the margins' have their own voice?
- How did you find the process of making of the piece?

Samuel and Chloe, from the company, graciously responded, in some detail, via a video message to the students. It became apparent that the two-way learning journey, as mentioned, was visible. FlawBored were able to contextualise their work, in their own words, and with agency, to nascent scholars in the academic space, thus confronting one of the themes of their piece—'able anxiety'—and proving that 'by listening to and respecting the voices of marginalised individuals, we can support them in taking greater control of their lives and challenge those who seek to exclude them' (Shevlin & Rose, 2022, p. 1). Creating valuable spaces for the marginalised to speak for themselves within the academy is intrinsic to this goal. The act of introducing their work to the project has resulted in *their* entry into the literature, not least via this paper, giving them some level of parity with other works deemed 'authoritative in our culture' (Bloom, 1994, p. 2). The students' learning journey was materially impacted by the knowledge that this sort of work was available and being (successfully) made. They were able to begin to understand that there was work in the professional sphere that thematically and structurally challenged and confronted issues that to them are just conversations or embodied experiences. Their attitude and willingness to partake in the project was markedly different after this interaction. A sense of purpose that existed beyond grades and marks was sparked. In coming face to face—or in this case, screen to screen—with the makers of such work, the students were able to see the theory of Boal (for example) made flesh; they could see what was, is, and could, be possible. It is argued that in introducing the work in a manner that did not remove it from the 'mainstream' but positioned it as work that could be accessed and therefore explored in the module, made this realisation more tangible—there was a currency in the contemporaneousness and exclusivity in working with this new text.

If we accept the idea that education exists to pose problems that students can relate to in real terms, we acknowledge that they 'will feel increasingly challenged and obliged to respond to that challenge [...] Their response to the challenge evokes new challenges, followed by new understandings; and gradually the students come to regard themselves as committed' (Freire, 2000, p. 81). This commitment is a precursor to dedicated independent and self-motivated study.

## BLUEPRINTS AND BUILDING

Once fully engaged with the piece, and with the beginnings of ideas around the social justice issues that they wished to explore, the students were tasked with reading the script three times.

The first read of any script, it is here suggested, should be reconnaissance, gaining a sense of *what* is happening. The second read should look to untangle *why* what happens does. The third read, the last before action, is to understand *how* what happens does. It is contended that encountering scripts in this way allows for the mind to work in the order that it encounters the world, seeing what is there before ascribing meaning—*'l'existence précède l'essence'* (Sartre, 1970, p. 36)—maybe this is an existential mode of thinking, but in a world seemly experiencing multiple existential crises, this perhaps seems apt.

After the first read, the students were able to recant the base narrative and the secondary story, after the second, the themes became more apparent and after the third, they began to understand and question the structure. Through prior learning, the concept of narrative cogency was something that they were familiar with. In reading, they, as politically aware individuals, began to form ideas of themes that they were interested in exploring. It was therefore clear that the best use of the text would be to mine it for structure, in the knowledge that '[w]ith practice, the process of structuring becomes instinctive' (Jeffreys, 2019, p.9) and that the use of a pre-existing example by an oppressed (or marginalised) group allows those who are marginalised to 'be their own example in the struggle for their redemption' (Freire, 2000, p. 54).

In groups, they were tasked to deconstruct each scene, with the aim of identifying what happened in each in broad terms, leading to the creation of a blueprint for their own work, this also facilitated them in understanding how and why the piece read and felt as it did. The uniqueness of the dramaturgical underpinning of the piece was achieved through honing over, possibly, hundreds of hours of work by FlawBored and whilst this method of mining is by no means a replacement for that dedicated work, it is a shortcut to the creation of a new piece of drama without the students losing their enthusiasm for the narrative and themes whilst 'creating' a new piece of social justice inspired drama. The aim was to facilitate engagement with social justice and not necessarily with ground-breaking and unseen new forms of theatrical presentation.

Culturing a preference to work in *Brave Spaces* which 'better prepare participants to interact authentically with one another in challenging dialogues' (Arao & Clemens, 2023, p. 149) over *Safe Spaces* which, due to the conflation of safety with comfort, do not 'foster a learning environment that supports participants in the challenging work with regard to issues of identity, oppression, power and privilege' (Arao & Clemens, 2023, pp. 138–139) allowed for, and facilitated, a level of sharpening of the students' own ideas with minimal external input. If we are to empower the makers of the future, we must give them the tools and see what it is that they make with them. To confront Beckett's famous statement: 'Ever tried. Ever failed. No matter. Try again. Fail again. Fail better' (Beckett, 1983), we must, in a supported and brave learning environment, allow mistakes to happen as 'one of the possible solutions to achieving more effective learning' (Lee, 2020, p. 9). If these moments of failure and/or doubt are understood to be 'precisely when new knowledge is created' (Lindgren Galloway, 2023, p. 19) empower-ment can be cemented pedagogically.

## LISTENING AND LEARNING

With a structure now in view, the students were tasked with exploring, in more depth, the social issues that they were interested in. It is important in this work to not impose assumptions but to create a shared learning space where students are able to bring their full selves and their personal interests to the work. The effect of this is to create a level of control and self-determination that such projects could fall foul of without such consideration; it also creates a space of true collaboration and learning for *all*.

Issues relating to geographical division, linguistic differences, cultural differences, challenging stereotypes, age, class, sexism, hierarchy, homophobia, technology, Politics, embodied and lived experience, expectations of young people, gender politics, and meta-theatre were identified and discussed by the group as a basis for their social justice foci—all of which challenge, directly, social norms. These interests align cogently with Baker and Ali's 2022 research in mapping young people's social justice concerns. These are issues that are reflective of where they are, and it is in these reflections that these specific young people needed to be met—there was learning for all in these important developmental discussions. Applied theatre can be understood to offer the 'potential to play with alternatives, and offer space for communities to engage with the politics of oppression' (Abraham, 2021, p. 4); this project stays true to this definition whilst also offering the tools to these students to disseminate these ideas through their acquired theatre making skills as they advance into their careers.

## MOTIVATION

With a structure and themes in hand, the focus now turned to the creation of the work that they would perform to their peers and staff. It was communally decided that instead of creating separate pieces tackling the vast array of issues identified separately, they would create one piece of theatre would allow for all of the themes to work with and against each other. In taking inspiration from FlawBored, the group centred the marginalised as opposed to pitting it against that which creates and services the marginalisation. In doing so, they began to take ownership of their *process* instead of being focussed on the *product*.

In rehearsing, the students were incredibly self-motivated as their ownership of the project and process created an intrinsic motivation (Hanrahan & Banerjee, 2017). In higher education spaces it can often be the case that themes are imposed from a position of hierarchical privilege—the opposite was the case here. Students were very much the thematic leads, with dramaturgical and skill acquisition input offered where and when useful. Harnessing this motivation is important not only in the pursuit of education but in the pursuit of self-determination and understanding, and claiming, of agency—a pre-requisite for social justice advocacy. In order to teach and study through, and with, a social justice lens, it is logical to embed social justice in its study; as the students looked to learn around metatheatrical principles from the source text, they could also learn from metasocial enaction in the learning.

## LESSONS LEARNED

The final performance, which was entitled 'Listen', comprised a series of thematically connected vignettes. Performatively, these oscillated between narrative based drama, metatheatrical scenes commenting on what went before and/or what was to come, and narrator lead, almost Brechtian inspired narrative interruptions. Thematically, they aimed to explore the social justice issues that the students had identified in their earlier work. Some scenes focussed on one theme whereas some explored, lightly, intersectionality and how the collision of issues can sometimes bring more nuanced discussion and discovery. Between these performed scenes were pre-recorded audio monologues. These aural monologues were all single voice and pulled on the theme of being sorry that things are the way that they are—something gleaned from the analysis of the FlawBored text. They were voiced by the writer in a confessional manner and allowed more themes to be touched upon than could be included in the 45-minute performance. Practically, this allowed for changing of set, and costume for the cast.

In their evaluative statements, the students commented on how much they enjoyed the process, identifying, in several instances, that the autonomy, and freedom, that they had was incredibly important, as was the ability to voice their thoughts and opinions in a space that not only welcomed them but acted upon them. It became apparent that some of the students had a deeper appreciation of their power, and indeed the power of theatre, in tackling and discussing pertinent and the sometimes thorny issues associated with such themes. In evaluative discussion each member of the group delineated something that they learned about themselves; words such as 'understood', 'felt', 'experienced', 'engaged' and 'surprised' were used repeatedly. Their worldview and/or the world hitherto unknown to them, became clear(er).

## CONCLUSION

If we are to seriously agitate for a better world, we are compelled to build the conditions for that better world to come into existence. This is very often more about *how* we do what we do, over and above what it *is* that we do. Creating a space for open and engaged inquiry into deeply help viewpoints which, in other spaces, could be shied away from, is one of the major bonuses of introducing professional, critically acclaimed, work to students at this point in their careers. Having the ability to converse with those makers makes the world feel smaller and therefore more approachable, engendering a sense of belonging for both sides.

The study of racism, sexism, homophobia and indeed ableism, should—and needs to be—accessible to the broadest range of voices. If we are to have nuanced discussions leading to sustainable and actionable change instead of narrowing, we can—and must—seek to broaden. This broadening—in educational circles at the very least—is reliant on the ability and willing of those who find themselves in positions of power and privilege to acknowledge their position before using it to the betterment of all who are, or could be, in their orbit. Looking outward necessitates acknowledging and laying open gaps in knowledge as well as the ambition and willing to face those gaps down and work with them instead of ignoring them. Doing nothing to create inclusion is arguably as good and as useful as actively raising barriers. To this end, broadening the canon to encompass a wider span of lived experience will only work if it is done, the canon is not an organic orgasm but one that is curated and kept, even Bloom acknowledges that '[w]riters, artists, composers themselves determine canons, by bridging between strong precursors and strong successors' (Bloom, 1994, p. 522)—if we continue to do the same things in the same ways, the same results will occur, and the same exclusions will perpetuate. We need to find different ways of bridging the gap. Looking to the margins, and the spaces in between, is often where richness lies. Fringe theatre can be a site of canonical growth.

The aim is not to remove, but to enrich, countering Bloom's unfounded assertion that there is an 'academic-journalistic network' who wish 'to overthrow the Canon in order to advance their supposed (and non-existent) programs for social change' (Bloom, 1994, p. 4).

Knowing that FlawBored's work sits within a rich mellifluous lineage of work that began life in fringe contexts, will give roots to the 'trees' that students will cultivate. They will care because it is theirs and they will own it because it is theirs. Freire's suggestion that when the oppressed 'discover within themselves the yearning to be free, they perceive that this yearning can be transformed into reality only when the same yearning is aroused in their comrades' (Freire, 2000, p. 47) is manifested here as (and in) the students' motivation. The care and ownership witnessed in this case study led to more engaged and engaging learning—there is absolutely no reason for this to not be the case in the other projects that this paper will hopefully inspire.

Connecting those in the profession to those in training allows for there to be a two-way learning journey, where the profession enriches those to come and those to come enrich the profession with new ideas and different provocations. Facilitating this through enacted critical pedagogy methodology ensures that there is a rigour in such work. In this way the profession will always be alert to what it is and what it could be, it would be continuously evolving and including—this can only be a good thing in the telling of our shared humanity.

Not once in this project was the phrase 'Applied Theatre' used, but there is little doubt that that is what this project was. The trick now, is to ensure that the learning and fervour engendered in this process is not dissipated by the adverse experiences that may lay ahead. We change the world one story at a time.

**SUGGESTED CITATION**

Daly, D. (2024). Social justice and fringe theatre in higher education. *ArtsPraxis, 11* (1), pp. 106-120.

**REFERENCES**

Abraham, N. (2021). Applied theatre: An introduction. In T. Prentki & N. Abraham (Eds.), *The applied theatre reader,* 2nd ed., pp. 3–9. Routledge.

Arao, B., & Clemens, K. (2023). From safe spaces to brave spaces. In *The art of effective facilitation*, pp. 135–150.

Baker, A., & Ali, L. (2022). Mapping young people's social justice concerns: An exploration of voice and action.

Beckett, S. (1983). *Worstward ho*. New York: Grove Press.

Bloom, H. (1994). *The Western Canon: The Books and School of the Ages*. New York: Harcourt Brace.

Boal, A. (2002). *Games for actors and non-actors*. Routledge.

Cameron, R. (2009). From *Great Women* to *Top Girls*: Pageants of sisterhood in British feminist theater. *Comparative Drama, 43* (2), pp. 143–166.

Churchill, C. (2018). *Top girls*. Bloomsbury Publishing.

*FlawBored | Home*. (n.d.). Flawbored.

Freire, P. (2000). *Pedagogy of the oppressed: 30th Anniversary Edition*. Continuum.

Gardner, L. (2021, October 4). Subsidised theatre's case for funding comes in showing how it differs from commercial. The Stage. Retrieved November 13, 2023.

Lindgren Galloway, S. (2023). Embracing failure in the drama classroom. *ArtsPraxis, 10* (2), pp. 16-31.

Hanrahan, F., & Banerjee, R. (2017). 'It makes me feel alive': the socio-motivational impact of drama and theatre on marginalised young people. *Emotional and Behavioural Difficulties*, 22 (1), pp. 35–49.

Hansberry, L. (2004). *A raisin in the sun*. Vintage.

*Jeffreys, S. (2019). Playwriting: Structure, character, how and what to write.* Nick Hern Books.

Lee, W. S. (2020). An experimental investigation into the application of a learning-from-mistakes approach among freshmen students. *SAGE Open, 10* (2).

Leeds Beckett University. (2022, September 22). Leeds Beckett University | Lift Off Festival 2022: Performing Arts and Theatre & Performance.

Lit in Colour | Penguin Random House. (2023, September 11).

Queer Folio — 1623 theatre company. (n.d.). 1623 Theatre Company.

Putnam, L. (2023, March 14). From *Fleabag* to *Six*: 7 shows launched by Edinburgh Fringe. *Playbill*.

Rodgers, J. (2022, March 7). Diversity School redacted report 2021.

Rose, T. (2014). Hansberry's *A Raisin in the Sun* and the "illegible"

politics of (inter)personal justice. *Kalfou*, pp. 27–60.
rxtheatre. (2020, June 24). *RXConnect panel event: House of Bernarda Alba* [Video]. YouTube.
Sartre, J. (1970). *L'existentialisme est un humanisme*. Nagel.
Sherman, M. (1998). *Bent: The play*. Hal Leonard Corporation.
Shevlin, M., & Rose, R. (2022). Respecting the voices of individuals from marginalised communities in research—"Who is listening and who isn't?" *Education Sciences, 12* (5), pp. 304.
Sterling, E. (2002). Bent straight: the destruction of self in Martin Sherman's *Bent*. *Journal of European Studies, 32* (127), pp. 369–388.
*What is Multiplay Drama?* (n.d.). Multiplay Drama.
*Who's working in HE?: Personal characteristics*. (2024, January 30). HESA.

**AUTHOR BIOGRAPHY**

Dermot Daly is a Senior Lecturer in the School of Drama at Leeds Conservatoire where he is also a member of the EDI Committee, he is also a Lecturer at Leeds School of Arts, Leeds Beckett University. His research interests include equality, diversity and inclusion; curriculum reform and implementation; widening participation; and practical drama/acting teaching methodology and practice.

# Reimagining Learning Spaces: The Rise of Theatrical Inquiry in Arts Education

### NICHOLAS WAXMAN

CREATIVE AGENCY LAB, ROYAL MELBOURNE INSTITUTE OF TECHNOLOGY

### ABSTRACT

*This paper explores the evolving concept of theatrical inquiry, tracing its origins, early applications, and its notable resurgence in recent years as a dynamic methodology for probing into learning spaces. Amidst the evolving landscape of arts education, theatrical inquiry endures as a lens through which the contemporary role of drama and theatre can be re-evaluated and redefined. This exploration is set against the backdrop of an ongoing debate: the demarcation between theatre-making and drama as pedagogical tools. By scrutinising the utility of theatrical inquiry in fostering aesthetic understanding and awareness amongst students, this study positions itself at the intersection of Drama in Education and Applied Theatre. It seeks to unravel the complexities of using drama and theatre not just as mediums of artistic expression but as critical instruments that can enhance cognitive, emotional, social, and creative reflection. Through a comprehensive review of literature, this paper aims to shed light on the varied ways in which theatrical inquiry can enrich arts education. It contributes to the academic discourse by providing a timeline of the evolution of the term theatrical inquiry and offers practical insights for educators looking to incorporate these approaches into their teaching practices in the arts.*

## BACKGROUND

Throughout arts-based research projects, the phrase 'theatrical inquiry' frequently appears, but its usage can significantly vary, leading to potential ambiguities regarding its meaning and application. It's important to clarify that merely juxtaposing the words 'theatrical' and 'inquiry' does not necessarily denote the employment of theatrical inquiry as a methodology. Often, researchers may refer to theatrical inquiry synonymously with concepts such as theatrical question, theatrical intent, processing theatre as a field, or even dramaturgy. This conflation of terms can obscure the distinct methodological framework that theatrical inquiry embodies.

In the vast landscape of arts-based research, theatrical inquiry is sometimes utilised to articulate the thematic or conceptual focus of a study, rather than its methodological approach. Such instances might see the term deployed to describe an investigation's dramaturgical underpinnings or to signify a project's overarching theatrical questions or intentions. While these are valid and valuable uses of the term within certain contexts, they diverge from the specific focus of this paper.

This exploration is dedicated to understanding theatrical inquiry in its capacity as a method or approach to research. This delineation is critical; as I am concerned with how theatrical inquiry can be operationalised as a rigorous, systematic methodology that leverages the unique perspectives and processes of theatre to inform and enrich the research endeavour. This paper does not address the broader, more colloquial uses of the term to describe the content or thematic focus of a study. Instead, we aim to illuminate how theatrical inquiry, as a distinct methodological approach, can offer profound insights and innovations within the realm of arts-based educational research.

By foregrounding this specific interpretation of theatrical inquiry, I seek to contribute to a more nuanced and focused dialogue. I am hoping this clarification allows us to delve deeply into the potentials and applications of theatrical inquiry in a way that is both methodically sound and creatively fruitful, setting a foundation for future research that distinctly recognises and utilises the methodology's unique contributions to the field of arts-based research.

## ENQUIRY VS. INQUIRY

The terms 'enquiry' and 'inquiry' are often used interchangeably, but they have subtle differences, especially in British English, which tends to distinguish between the two. 'Enquiry' typically refers to the act of asking for information, a general query or question. It is often used in everyday contexts where someone is seeking knowledge or clarification. 'Inquiry,' on the other hand, denotes a more formal investigation, often with a systematic approach to uncovering facts or understanding deeper issues.

In this paper, 'inquiry' is chosen over 'enquiry' to emphasise the formal, methodological nature of the investigation. 'Theatrical inquiry' thus signifies a structured, rigorous approach to research, leveraging the unique methods and insights of theatre to delve into specific research questions. This choice underscores the systematic and methodological focus of the exploration, aligning with the academic and investigative rigor required in arts-based educational research. By clarifying these terms, we aim to avoid potential ambiguities and ensure a precise understanding of the methodological framework discussed in this paper.

## HISTORICAL CONTEXT AND EVOLUTION

The term 'theatrical inquiry' has been traced back to the early 19th century, marking its presence in the academic and cultural discourse as early as 1813. The term was used once in "The Theatrical Inquisitor, Or, Monthly Mirror" (1813) as it explored the nature of inquiry into theatrical endeavours. "The Theatrical Inquisitor, Or, Monthly Mirror," was a pivotal publication in the early 19th century, focusing on the vibrant world of theatre. It emerged as a crucial platform for reviews, critiques, and discussions, delving into the performances, actors, and dramatic works of the era. Through its pages, the periodical offered a selection of poetry, critical essays, and articles that engaged with the theatrical arts, serving both as a mirror to the practices of the time and as an inquisitor into the evolving dynamics of performance and stagecraft. This publication held a significant place in the cultural landscape of the time, scrutinising the theatre scene with a discerning eye and providing insights that were both informative and provocative. Its contribution to the discourse on theatre and performance underscored the importance of critical engagement and reflection in the arts, marking it as a seminal reference point for those interested in the depths and breadths of theatrical expression and critique.

Initially, the term 'theatrical inquiry' served as a critical tool for dissecting the narrative structures and cultural nuances within both new and traditional theatre movements. Early scholarly and journalistic efforts, as noted by Bigsby (1985), Gordon (1990), and Reason (2008), primarily applied theatrical inquiry to dissect narrative structures and cultural idiosyncrasies within both new and traditional theatre movements. The scope of theatrical inquiry broadened with scholars like Sohn (2011), Mendez (2014), and Horley (2014), exploring wider themes and principles within the theatre.

Sohn (2011) introduces "Western frames of theatrical inquiry" (p. 24), pointing towards a cultural and methodological context. Sohn's use of the term "Western frames of theatrical inquiry" subtly implies the presence of an established yet undefined methodology within the realm of Western theatre studies. This phraseology, while not uncommon in scholarly discussions, suggests a broad, somewhat nebulous conception of theatrical inquiry as it is practiced and understood in Western contexts. Sohn's use of this term highlights a broader academic trend where theatrical inquiry often becomes a catch-all phrase, encompassing a wide array of theatrical and dramaturgical pursuits without delving into the specificities of methodology, focus, or theoretical underpinnings. The invocation of Western frames of theatrical inquiry by Sohn highlights an assumption of a coherent, if not fully articulated, methodological approach that underlies Western theatrical analysis and critique. This presumed methodology encompasses the diverse practices, analytical techniques, and interpretative strategies that have been developed and employed within Western theatre and performance studies. However, by not delineating the contours of this methodology, the term leaves open questions about what precisely constitutes these frames of inquiry and how they differentiate from or intersect with non-Western approaches. Furthermore, Sohn's reference to Western frames of theatrical inquiry implicitly critiques the homogenisation of theatrical studies under a Western paradigm, suggesting a need for greater specificity and clarity in how these methodological approaches are defined, challenged, and expanded. It underscores the importance of acknowledging the diversity within Western theatrical traditions themselves, as well as the necessity of incorporating a wider range of cultural, aesthetic, and philosophical perspectives into the discourse. This perspective calls for a re-examination of the assumptions that underlie "Western frames of theatrical inquiry," advocating for an approach that is both more inclusive and more reflective of the globalised nature of contemporary theatre.

Mendez (2014) engages with the term theatrical inquiry in their analysis of Shakespeare's works, introducing a nuanced layer to the understanding of this concept, particularly in the context of literary and dramaturgical analysis. By examining Shakespeare's plays, Mendez illuminates how themes of love, the supernatural, and the psychiatric are explored through a lens of "poetic and theatrical inquiry" (p. 78), thereby underscoring the depth and complexity of Shakespeare's engagement with these themes across his body of work. This approach suggests that "theatrical inquiry" encompasses not only the methods by which theatre and performance are created and interpreted but also the ways in which these artistic forms probe into the human condition, society, and the broader cosmos of knowledge and understanding. Mendez's use of theatrical inquiry does what many scholarly discussions tend to overlook: it highlights the intrinsic relationship between the content of Shakespeare's plays and the process of inquiry itself. The term, as used by Mendez, implies a dynamic and exploratory process that Shakespeare employs to navigate and interrogate the myriad themes within his plays. It suggests that Shakespeare's works serve as a conduit for a broader investigation into the nature of human experience, leveraging the theatrical form as a means of delving into the complexities of life, emotion, and the unseen forces that shape our world. Furthermore,

Mendez's invocation of theatrical inquiry within the analysis of Shakespeare's plays calls attention to the dramatist's methodological approach to knowledge acquisition and dissemination. The question posed by Mendez, regarding the sources of Shakespeare's extensive knowledge, points to the poet's masterful synthesis of information from ancient and modern sources, filtered through the lens of his dramatic art. This synthesis, Mendez suggests, is not merely a matter of literary scholarship but a form of theatrical inquiry that engages with and expands upon the information and themes it encompasses. By framing Shakespeare's exploration of themes within the context of theatrical inquiry, Mendez contributes to a broader understanding of the term as a reflective and investigative process inherent in the creation and interpretation of theatre. This perspective encourages readers and scholars alike to consider the ways in which theatrical and poetic works not only reflect but actively engage with and question the world around them. Mendez's analysis thus positions theatrical inquiry as a crucial component of Shakespeare's artistic oeuvre, one that underpins his enduring relevance and the continued fascination with his works. In essence, Mendez's discussion of theatrical inquiry in relation to Shakespeare's plays challenges the academic community to view "theatrical inquiry" not just as a methodological tool but as an integral aspect of the creative process itself. This approach opens up new avenues for understanding the interplay between theatre, poetry, and the pursuit of knowledge, highlighting the role of artistic expression as a form of profound inquiry into the human experience.

Horley (2014) focuses on the audience's perspective, notably "placing the female at the centre of theatrical inquiry" (p. 22), which shifts the lens towards gender dynamics and audience engagement. Horley employs the term "theatrical inquiry" in a manner that illuminates their perspective on the transformative power of theatre to challenge and redefine societal norms, particularly concerning gender dynamics. By focusing on Franca Rame's monologues, which centralise the female experience within the context of theatrical exploration, Horley highlights how theatrical inquiry can serve as a potent tool for political and social critique. Rame's work, as interpreted by Horley, leverages the theatrical form not merely as a medium for storytelling but as a platform for engaging in deeper socio-political discourse, positioning the female perspective at the heart of this inquiry. This use of theatrical inquiry underscores the capacity of theatre to interrogate and dismantle prevailing gender constructs, offering an alternative to traditional narratives that often relegate female characters to the periphery or define them primarily in relation to male desire. Horley suggests that by placing the female voice at the centre of theatrical inquiry, Rame's monologues do more than just tell women's stories; they actively challenge the audience to reconsider and critique the male-dominated lens through which society frequently views and values women. Furthermore, Horley's reference to theatrical inquiry as a politically motivated act underscores the notion that theatre can be a form of activism, a means of questioning and potentially altering the status quo. In this context, theatrical inquiry is not just an academic or artistic pursuit but a deliberate act of resistance against entrenched societal norms and a call to think differently about gender, power, and representation.

Kear (2013) expands the concept of theatrical inquiry by moving beyond the cerebral into the physical. Kear's approach to theatrical inquiry, exemplified through their analysis of a waiter's mishap in a restaurant, underscores the potential of this methodology to dissect and understand real moments in life and the genuine experiences of individuals. This incident, seemingly minor in the grand scheme of things, is elevated by Kear to illustrate how theatrical inquiry can be applied to everyday occurrences, suggesting a broader applicability to a range of real-life situations. By situating "a seemingly inconsequential occurrence...as the site of a theatrical inquiry into the relations of presentation and representation structuring the situation itself and governing its emergence as a moment of historical transition" (Kear, 2013, p. 28), Kear posits that these moments are ripe for analysis, offering insights into the social fabric that constitutes human interaction. The implication of Kear's methodology suggests that theatrical inquiry can serve as a lens through which the intricacies of real-life experiences are examined, revealing the layered dynamics of presentation—how individuals portray themselves and are perceived in social contexts—and representation—the ways in which these portrayals are interpreted or narrated within the broader cultural narrative. This framework allows for a deep dive into how individuals navigate their roles within society, how they are affected by and affect the perceptions of others, and how these interactions contribute to or reflect larger societal narratives and transitions. Applying theatrical inquiry to real-life experiences enables a nuanced exploration of the performative aspects of everyday life, where every interaction, every encounter, can be seen as a performance imbued with meaning, waiting to be interpreted. It acknowledges that personal experiences are not isolated incidents but are embedded within a network of social relations and cultural contexts, each carrying the potential to inform our understanding of societal norms, values, and shifts. Furthermore, Kear's approach invites researchers and practitioners to consider how moments of conflict, misunderstanding, or transition in ordinary life can serve as windows into the human condition, offering valuable perspectives on identity, power dynamics, and social change. It challenges us to view our own experiences and those of others not just as happenings but as performances laden with cultural significance, thereby broadening the scope of theatrical inquiry to encompass the breadth of human experience. In essence, Kear (2013) provides a compelling argument for the expansive potential of theatrical inquiry to analyze and interpret the real experiences of people. This methodology does not limit itself to the realm of theatre and performance in the conventional sense but extends to the theatre of everyday life, where every action, every interaction, carries the weight of performance, each with its own story to tell and lesson to impart about the human experience.

## INTERDISCIPLINARY SHIFTS

Gardner (2000) delves into the complexities of theatrical inquiry, utilizing Artaud's "Un athlétisme affectif" as a case study to explore the broader implications of method and technique within theatre studies. "Un athlétisme affectif" translates to "an affective athleticism" in English. This phrase, often associated with the work of Antonin Artaud, a French playwright, poet, actor, and theatre director, emphasizes the physical and emotional exertion involved in performance. Artaud was a key figure in the early 20th century avant-garde theatre and the Theatre of Cruelty, a movement that sought to break away from traditional theatre forms and conventions to affect audiences deeply and viscerally. In the context of Artaud's philosophy, "un athlétisme affectif" refers to the rigorous, intense physical and emotional engagement that actors should bring to their performances. It suggests that actors must undergo a kind of training or discipline that is not just physical but also deeply emotional, enabling them to express profound and primal feelings through their bodies and voices. This concept is part of Artaud's broader vision for a theatre that impacts audiences on a deep, affective level, challenging them to confront their own emotions and subconscious.

In Gardner's analysis of Artaud conceptualisation of inquiry, Gardner identifies a crucial aspect of theatrical inquiry: the tension between the specificity of acting techniques and the expansive potential of theatre to engage with wide-ranging cultural critiques. Gardner articulates, "This is partly a consequence of the effect produced by the text of 'Un athletisme affectif,' and partly a result of [the author's] general strategy of developing wide-ranging critiques from apparently narrow topics" (Gardner, 2000, p. 11). Through this observation, Gardner highlights how theatrical inquiry often transcends the immediate concerns of actor training to touch upon broader cultural and theatrical discussions.

Gardner's critique emphasizes the importance of viewing theatrical inquiry not as a limitation to actor-focused discourse but as an opportunity to explore the multifaceted role of theatre within cultural contexts. He points out that the seeming vagueness or indirection in discussions about theatre methods can, in fact, open up a richer field of inquiry that challenges traditional boundaries and encourages a more holistic understanding of theatre's impact. According to Gardner, "[the author's] discussion...moves within and across a much larger field of cultural as well as theatrical inquiry" (Gardner, 2000, p. 11), suggesting that the value of theatrical inquiry lies in its ability to navigate and connect diverse thematic terrains.

Furthermore, Gardner suggests that the perceived absence of concrete methods in theatrical texts should not be seen as a shortfall but rather as an invitation for readers to engage more deeply with the underlying visions and metaphors, constructing meaning from the broader implications of the work. This approach underscores Gardner's view that theatrical inquiry is a dynamic and interpretive process, one that enriches our understanding of theatre by prompting us to look beyond the surface of technique and performance, and to consider the wider cultural and philosophical questions that theatre raises.

In essence, Gardner (2000) redefines the scope of theatrical inquiry, advocating for an approach that embraces the complexity and ambiguity inherent in theatre studies. By focusing on the broader implications of theatrical inquiry, Gardner contributes to a nuanced discourse on the role of theatre as a medium for cultural critique and exploration, highlighting the importance of interpretive and analytical engagement in the study of theatre.

A significant shift occurred with Biehl's 2008 paper, which repositioned theatrical inquiry as an interdisciplinary method. This approach broadened the scope of inquiry to encompass the aesthetics of social and organisational phenomena, moving beyond the confines of traditional theatre studies. Biehl's emphasis on 'sensual perception' and the bodily experiences in performance situations introduced a new dimension to theatrical inquiry, suggesting that even everyday interactions could be analysed through the lens of 'theatrical communication.' This perspective opened up new avenues for exploring the role of theatre in society, extending the applicability of theatrical inquiry to a wider range of contexts.

Recent contributions from Diaz (2020) have further enriched the discourse around theatrical inquiry, infusing it with elements of 'cultural inquiry.' Their work has expanded the framework of theatrical inquiry, integrating it with broader cultural and educational research agendas. This evolution marks a move towards a more holistic understanding of theatre's role in education, particularly within the context of Arts-Based Educational Research.

Diaz (2020) delves into theatrical inquiry through the lens of how theatre can catalyse social reflection and transformation without resorting to didacticism or propaganda. This exploration is grounded in the critique of past approaches where theatre was constrained by political agendas, limiting its scope and impact. Diaz cites Uribe's perspective that theatre's role is not to dictate thoughts or actions but to foster a space for questioning and engaging with history. This shift away from propagandistic content allowed for a resurgence in the expressive potential of theatre, marrying political engagement with artistic freedom. By staging performances in a university setting as a process of theatrical inquiry and choosing to leave the performance "in the rough," Diaz highlights a deliberate move towards fostering a more dynamic interaction between the performers and the audience (Diaz, 2020, p. 82).

The specific case of the Orwell play '1984' is used to exemplify how theatrical inquiry can illuminate social divisions and historical narratives that are often marginalized or ignored by mainstream discourse. Rather than aiming to alter the political landscape directly, the play seeks to contribute to a broader awareness and understanding of Colombia's social fissures and the historical context. Through this analysis, Diaz (2020) articulates a vision of theatrical inquiry that extends beyond the confines of traditional theatre, advocating for a form of performance that is both reflective and engaging. This approach suggests that theatre, by embracing its inherent capacity for inquiry and expression, can play a significant role in societal discourse, not by offering solutions but by highlighting questions and histories that prompt deeper contemplation and understanding among its audience.

## EMERGING ELEMENTS OF THEATRICAL INQUIRY

The foundations of theatrical inquiry as a methodology are deeply rooted in the interdisciplinary confluence of theatre studies, education, and cultural analysis, framing theatre not just as an art form but as a potent medium for exploration and transformation. This methodological approach harnesses the unique aspects of theatre — such as performance, narrative engagement, and audience interaction — to delve into and illuminate complex social, cultural, and pedagogical phenomena. The theoretical basis of theatrical inquiry suggests that theatre's inherent processes and principles offer insightful perspectives on human experiences, societal structures, and educational practices (Gardner, 2000; Horley, 2014).

Central to theatrical inquiry is the notion that theatre serves as a lens through which the world can be understood and interrogated. This belief in theatre's capacity to uncover societal truths through storytelling, character exploration, and emotional engagement posits it as an unparalleled medium for examining the human condition. Theatrical inquiry allows for the investigation of narrative construction, identity formation, and the reinforcement or disruption of societal norms, providing a unique platform for critical examination and dialogue (Mendez, 2014; Sohn, 2011).

The methodological framework of theatrical inquiry is distinguished by its focus on active participation and engagement, challenging the traditional research paradigms that may prioritize objectivity and detachment. This approach advocates for a deeply immersive experience in the subject matter, fostering a dynamic interplay among researchers, participants, and the theatrical content. Such engagement with theatre-making and performance invites a collaborative creation of meaning, effectively merging theory with practice and eroding the boundaries between observer and participant (Kear, 2013).

Incorporating a critical pedagogical lens, theatrical inquiry views education as a transformative space where drama and performance act as catalysts for empowerment. Influenced by educational theorists advocating for engaged, reflective learning, this methodology positions drama as a tool for questioning prevailing narratives, exploring diverse perspectives, and catalyzing change within educational contexts (Freeman et al., 2003; Widdows, 1996).

Affect studies also significantly inform the theoretical foundation of theatrical inquiry, emphasizing the integral role of emotions and sensory experiences in shaping understanding and interactions. This focus on the affective dimensions of theatre enhances the research process, allowing for a comprehensive exploration that incorporates both intellectual and emotional responses, thereby enriching the depth and empathy of the engagement (Gregg & Seigworth, 2010; Harris, 2021).

Theatrical inquiry, grounded in the synthesis of insights from theatre studies, critical pedagogy, and affect studies, presents a novel and enriching approach to research. This methodology values creativity, emotional resonance, and participatory engagement, offering a profound way to engage with educational, cultural, and social inquiries. Through the application of theatrical principles to broader research endeavours, theatrical inquiry fosters innovative perspectives and transformative learning experiences (Gardner, 2000; Horley, 2014; Mendez, 2014; Sohn, 2011; Kear, 2013).

## THEATRICAL INQUIRY IN EDUCATIONAL SETTINGS

The nuanced exploration of theatrical inquiry within educational settings, especially through drama's potent role in amplifying student engagement and agency, unfolds as a multifaceted dialogue that underscores the profound impact of integrating this approach into educational frameworks. As delineated through the collective insights of scholars, drama's intersection with affect studies and creative agency heralds a transformative shift in educational paradigms, from traditional, teacher-centered models to dynamic, student-driven environments that prioritize emotional engagement and participatory learning.

The participatory essence of drama, underscored by Heffernan & Wilkinson (2023) and Harris (2021), transcends conventional pedagogical methods by fostering a learning atmosphere that privileges the student's emotional and sensory experiences. This shift from passive absorption to active engagement in the learning process is not merely a pedagogical preference but a critical response to the evolving needs of students in contemporary educational landscapes. Drama, in this context, becomes a conduit for the circulation of affect, providing a platform where students can exercise their creative agency, thereby cultivating a sense of ownership and personal investment in their educational trajectories.

The capacity of drama to provide students with a voice and a platform for expression is particularly significant in the context of fostering inclusivity within the classroom. The perspectives of Literat (2021) and Stephenson (2023), alongside the foundational theories of Gregg & Seigworth (2010), illuminate how drama serves as a critical medium for enabling students to articulate their perspectives and engage with content in a manner that is deeply affective and personally meaningful. This form of engagement is crucial in creating an educational environment where all students, irrespective of their backgrounds or learning styles, feel valued, heard, and emotionally connected to their learning experience.

Furthermore, the integration of drama in education as a potent tool for social and emotional learning embodies the principles of creative agency. Engaging students in role-play and dramatic activities allows them to explore complex social situations and emotional landscapes in a safe, controlled setting. Such experiential learning, as highlighted by scholars like Widdows (1996) and Freeman et al. (2003), not only enhances social skills and empathy but also aligns with the goals of affect studies by fostering emotional intelligence. This approach reflects a holistic understanding of education, where the development of affective and interpersonal skills is regarded as equally important as cognitive achievements.

The diversity and dynamism of methodological approaches in drama education research further enrich the discourse on theatrical inquiry's role in schools. The use of qualitative methodologies and arts-based research methods, as explored by Bartone (2012) and Norris (2016), offers tools for delving into the nuanced experiences of drama in educational settings. These methodologies underscore the importance of capturing the subjective, experiential dimensions of drama, thereby providing a deeper understanding of its impact on student engagement and agency.

The application of drama in addressing broader educational concerns, such as curriculum development and inclusivity, places drama education at the forefront of pedagogical innovation. The challenges and opportunities of integrating arts into the standard curriculum, as discussed by Lee et al. (2015) and Harris and Holman Jones (2023), reflect the ongoing dialogue between creative, student-centered learning and the constraints of standardized testing. Drama's role in catering to diverse learning needs and fostering an inclusive educational experience further highlights its significance in meeting the diverse demands of contemporary education.

Finally, the exploration of student voice and agency within educational settings marks a paradigmatic shift towards empowering students in the learning process. The work of Charteris and Smardon (2019) and the foundational ideas of Dewey (1922) and Vygotsky (1978) emphasize the critical role of student participation in shaping their educational environments. This shift necessitates a revaluation of traditional educational roles and structures, advocating for a more inclusive, democratic approach that values student-driven innovation and engagement.

In essence, the deeper integration of theatrical inquiry and drama into educational frameworks represents a strategic and methodologically sound approach to enhancing the educational experience. By weaving together the principles of affect studies, creative agency, and methodological innovations in drama education research, this approach fosters a responsive and engaging learning environment. This environment not only supports the emotional and experiential dimensions of learning but also actively involves students in co-creating their educational journey, thereby laying the groundwork for a more engaged, reflective, and inclusive educational landscape.

## WHAT IS THEATRICAL INQUIRY IN 2024?

Theatrical inquiry, as elucidated through the cited literature and discussions, emerges as a multifaceted methodology that extends far beyond the traditional boundaries of theatre studies to encompass a broad spectrum of pedagogical, cultural, and social investigations. This methodology is characterized by its dynamic application across various contexts, its interdisciplinary nature, and its capacity to foster deep engagement, critical reflection, and transformative learning experiences.

At its core, theatrical inquiry is defined by its rigorous, systematic approach that leverages the unique perspectives and processes of theatre to inform and enrich research endeavors. This is not limited to the analysis of performances or the study of dramaturgy but extends to the exploration of how theatrical frameworks can illuminate complex social, cultural, and educational phenomena. The broad application of theatrical inquiry, as seen in the works of scholars such as Horley (2014), Sohn (2011), and Mendez (2014), demonstrates its versatility in addressing gender dynamics, cultural contexts, and the nuances of literary analysis within and beyond the confines of traditional theatre settings.

The interdisciplinary shifts highlighted by Gardner (2000) and the engagement with broader educational concerns underscore the relevance of theatrical inquiry within educational institutions. By bridging the gap between theatre studies and pedagogical theory, theatrical inquiry offers innovative approaches to curriculum development, teaching methodologies, and student engagement. This methodology supports the creation of learning environments where students can actively participate in their education, employing drama as a tool to explore identities, narratives, and social issues in a manner that fosters empathy, creativity, and critical thinking.

Central to the methodology of theatrical inquiry is its capacity to engage participants in reflective and meaningful ways. This engagement is often facilitated through the participatory nature of drama, which can encourage students to take an active role in their learning. The principles of creative agency and affect studies can be embodied through theatrical inquiry, providing platforms for participants to express their perspectives and engage with content on both intellectual and emotional levels. This approach can enhance emotional and sensory engagement within the educational process. According to Horley (2014), theatre has the potential to challenge and redefine societal norms, which can foster an inclusive environment where participants feel heard and valued.

Theatrical inquiry as a methodology is distinguished by its ability to facilitate a deeper understanding of and engagement with the world through the lens of theatre. It operates on the premise that theatrical processes and principles can offer profound insights into human experiences, societal structures, and educational practices. By adopting and adapting theatrical inquiry within educational settings, educators and researchers can unlock new dimensions of learning and understanding, creating spaces that promote inclusivity, critical reflection, and active participation. This methodology, therefore, stands as a testament to the enduring relevance and transformative potential of theatre in contemporary society and education.

The adoption of theatrical inquiry as a cornerstone for future interdisciplinary research holds significant potential. By foregrounding the lived experiences and voices of students, this approach can contribute to a deeper and more empathetic understanding of the educational landscape. The pioneering use of theatrical inquiry in this manner aspires to inspire further academic inquiry, encouraging researchers to explore the intersections between theatre, education, and phenomenology.

In conclusion, the exploration of theatrical inquiry from its historical roots to its contemporary applications in educational research reveals a field of study that is ripe with potential. By extending and adapting theatrical inquiry to new contexts, this term may contribute to the academic discourse and offers practical insights for enhancing the educational experience. The integration of theatrical inquiry into ABER represents a significant step forward, promising to enrich our understanding of education through the lens of theatre and performance.

**SUGGESTED CITATION**

Waxman, N. (2024). Re*imagining* learning spaces: The rise of theatrical inquiry in arts education. *ArtsPraxis, 11* (1), pp. 121-139.

**REFERENCES**

Barone, T., & Eisner, E. W. (2012). *Arts based research*. SAGE.
Biehl, B. (2008). The performance of women and men in organisations:

a theatre studies approach. *Gender in Management, 23* (7), pp. 522–527.

Bigsby, C. W. E. (1985). *A critical introduction to twentieth-century American drama: volume 3, beyond Broadway*. Kiribati: Cambridge University Press.

Cartocci, C. (2023). *The rise of the concept of "the theatrical" outside the performative arts*. Master's Thesis, Ca' Foscari University.

Charteris, J., & Smardon, D. (2019). Democratic contribution or information for reform? Prevailing and emerging discourses of student voice. *The Australian Journal of Teacher Education, 44* (6), pp. 1–18.

Dewey, J. (1922). Human nature and conduct, Vol. 14. *The middle works, 1899-1924*. Carbondale, IL: Southern Illinois University Press.

Dewey, J. (1938). The determination of ultimate values or aims through antecedent or a priori speculation or through pragmatic or empirical inquiry. *Teachers College Record: The Voice of Scholarship in Education, 39* (10), pp. 471–485.

Diaz Cardona, N. (2020). *The denied happiness: Stages of violence, terror and repression in Colombia*. Doctoral dissertation, Auckland University of Technology.

Diaz, E. (2020). Theatrical inquiry and cultural reflection. *Journal of Arts-Based Educational Research, 14* (2), pp. 72-85.

Freeman, G. D., Sullivan, K., & Fulton, C. R. (2003). Effects of creative drama on self-concept, social skills, and problem behavior. *The Journal of Educational Research*, 96 (3), pp. 131–138.

Gardner, A. P. (2000). *Antonin Artaud's 'affective athleticism': The development of a modern performance theory*. ProQuest One Academic. Doctoral Dissertation, The University of Manchester.

Gardner, L. (2000). Un athletisme affectif: Theatrical inquiry and cultural critique. *Theatre Journal, 52* (1), pp. 10-25.

Gordon, R. S. (1990). The Italian futurist theatre: A reappraisal. *The Modern Language Review, 85* (2), pp. 349–361.

Harris, D. X., & Holman Jones, S. (2023). A creative ecological approach to supporting young people with mental health challenges in schools. *International Journal of Qualitative Studies in Education, 37* (2), pp. 372-383.

Heffernan, J., & Wilkinson, L. (2023). Drama and student engagement: The role of affective learning. *Educational Theatre Journal, 55*

(3), pp. 201-216.

Horley, R. (2014). *An inquiry into the relevance of the practices of Commedia Dell'Arte to contemporary feminist theatre making*. Master's Thesis, University of Huddersfield.

Kear, A. (2013). *Theatre and event: Staging the European century*. Palgrave Macmillan.

Lee, B. K., Patall, E. A., Cawthon, S. W., & Steingut, R. R. (2015). The effect of drama-based pedagogy on pre-K–16 outcomes: A meta-analysis of research from 1985 to 2012. *Review of Educational Research, 85* (1), pp. 3-49.

Literat, I. (2021). Drama as a medium for student voice and agency. *Journal of Drama Education, 27* (4), pp. 455-469.

Méndez, S. (2016). Shakespeare's knowledge of imagination. *Complutense Journal of English Studies, 24*, pp. 61–87.

Norris, J. (2016). Drama as research: Realizing the potential of drama in education as a research methodology. *Youth Theatre Journal, 30* (2), pp. 122-135.

Reason, M. (2008). Thinking theatre: Enhancing children's theatrical experiences through philosophical inquiry. *Childhood & Philosophy, 7*, pp. 115–145.

Sohn, W. J. (2011). *In search of another eye: Mimesis, Chinese aesthetics, post/modern theatre*. Doctoral Dissertation, University of London.

Stephenson, P. (2023). Integrating drama in inclusive classrooms. *Arts Education Policy Review, 124* (2), pp. 150-165.

*The Theatrical Inquisitor, Or, Monthly Mirror*. (1813). United Kingdom: Chapple.

Vygotsky, L. S. (1978). *Mind in society: The development of higher psychological processes*. Cambridge, MA: Harvard University Press.

Widdows, J. (1996). Drama as an agent for change: Drama, behaviour and students with emotional and behavioural difficulties. *Research in Drama Education, 1* (1), pp. 65-78.

Wright, D. (2007). Constructivist inquiry and learning in drama. *NJ: Drama Australia Journal, 31* (1), pp. 45–54.

**AUTHOR BIOGRAPHY**

Nick Waxman is an award-winning Australian teacher, director and playwright who hosts *The Aside Podcast*, a free podcast for drama teachers. He is currently the Curriculum Resources Manager for three State Government Projects (Blended Arts Project, Next Stage Project & Positive Start Project). Nick serves on the board of Drama Victoria and Fusion Theatre, and is completing his PhD at RMIT in embodied drama in learning environments. As the Head of Theatre, Dance and Drama at Haileybury College he directs a season of musicals, plays and performances; in 2023 his creative direction of *The SpongeBob Musical* work was nominated 26 times.

ArtsPraxis
Volume 11 Issue 1
© 2024

# Praxis: The Application of Teaching and Deep Learning Strategies for the DBI Education Practitioner/Researcher

**BRENDA BURTON**

THE UNIVERSITY OF TEXAS AT TYLER

## ABSTRACT

*This literature review analyzes concepts about education, how we teach, and the nature of how students learn, full of applied learning theory as well as applied teaching theory. Discussions about transferring knowledge to novel situations (National Research Council, U.S., 2012) and applying those theories to instructional design (Khalil & Elkhider, 2016) create a welcomed perspective on the praxis of teaching, especially for the Drama-Based Instruction (DBI) education practitioner interested in iterative praxis improvement research. This article focuses on deep versus surface learning, applying instructional design for effective teaching, and the pursuit of depth of knowledge for competency beyond the classroom.*

The study of teaching and learning is a complex undertaking. Philosophy, theory, and practical application combine to inform the teaching praxis of educators. Concepts such as surface versus deep learning, psychological influences on pedagogy, and awareness of others' needs are important for insight into instructional practices and designs. From Socrates, Aristotle, and Plato to Piaget, Vygotsky, and the modern practitioner, much thought and research has gone in to improving education over time. Learning theories and teaching strategies have been analyzed to create understanding and epistemological paradigms have influenced how instructors hope to inspire and motivate their students. Learning about learning, as well as teaching, within an improvement paradigm is beneficial to the Drama-Based Instruction (DBI) education practitioner/researcher and provides a pathway to helping students reach successful outcomes. Praxis, or the combination of theory and practice, along with an understanding of teaching and learning, allows the DBI practitioner to connect with students for improved learning.

## DRAMA-BASED INSTRUCTION

Drama-Based Instruction (DBI) techniques, which include improvisation, interactive games, and role-playing techniques (such as Dorothy Heathcote's Mantle of the Expert), allow teachers to motivate their students and engage in authentic instruction (Cawthon et al., 2011). Cawthon et al. (*ibid.*) define student engagement as active participation in classroom activities and authentic instruction as that which utilizes such activities so that students may build on previous knowledge, think critically, and experience the application of collaboratively constructed knowledge. Additionally, DBI integrates into the curriculum so that a safe, scaffolded environment is democratically created by both teachers and students to actively create knowledge (*ibid.*) When students are thus engaged, self-efficacy and successful outcomes are likely to increase. DBI is a powerful tool in efforts to motivate and help students to achieve (Kyrimi & Tsiaras, 2021). The use of drama in education makes a compelling case for helping students to learn more deeply and apply the knowledge they create to identify real-world problems, evaluate potential solutions, and evaluate possible outcomes if applied (Aitken, 2013). Now more than ever, educators must find ways to help students that need it the most.

## THE NATURE OF STUDENT LEARNING

Biggs (1987) establishes a well-researched classification of how students learn. Having developed, employed, evaluated, and revised an instrument (e.g., questionnaire) to gather data in several domains regarding student learning, Biggs (*ibid*.) remained adaptable and improved his instrument in subsequent iterations. His resulting findings reveal internal and external orientations as predictors for how students approach learning. This orientation forecasts a tendency toward surface or deep learning. Biggs' three classifications or approaches to learning are: surface, deep, and achieving, each of which comprises motive and strategy (*ibid*.). In thinking about how students approach their understanding of what the education practitioner is trying to teach them, instructors will call to mind individual students in particular and will develop a new understanding of how those students, in the context of these classifications, relate to motive and strategy (*ibid*.).

When employing DBI, the teacher provides an experience whereby students learn to cooperate, develop self-confidence, and hone problem-solving skills (Kyrimi & Tsiaras, 2021). As Biggs (1987) noted, the three approaches may be combined (surface-achieving, deep-achieving, and though less likely, surface then deep successively, such as when an actor memorizes lines but then evaluates them for meaning) (*ibid*.). author also points out that intention is a critical piece of the puzzle. What a student intends for his or her own learning will determine the approach they adopt, even if it is not a conscious choice. This is often correlated to whether the student interacts in an external or internal manner with their learning environment (*ibid*.), especially in DBI. This recalls the Behaviorist vs. Cognitive theorist divide (think Pavlos vs. knowledge building) and how the learner's approach will impact teaching (Schunk, 2020). When applied as an instructional strategy (in DBI for example) the teacher may lead the student to construct their own meaning (Kauchak & Eggen, 2012). Biggs' descriptions of surface, deep, and achieving approaches to learning should be a valuable foundation for helping students learn more deeply and for competence.

## PERSPECTIVE ON DEEPER LEARNING

The fourth chapter of the National Research Council text (edited by Pellegrino and Hilton) on the nature of deeper learning emphasizes the need to develop 21st century competencies, and looks at how to use deep learning to "transfer" learned knowledge to be able to adapt and solve novel problems that arise. Because technology is increasingly replacing routine skills, we must also teach skills in innovation and how to creatively solve problems in order to advance. While specific transfer of learning generally requires common elements and general transfer of learning usually fails across disciplines, deep learning may be effective in using transfer to solve problems whereas rote learning is not (National Research Council, U.S., 2012). DBI techniques reinforce this notion as authentic instruction is emphasized even in poorer schools where resources are typically limited and where practices often rely on simple rote memorization, and allow the students to engage in actual participatory inquiry instead (Cawthon et al., 2011).

The National Research Council editors also reinforce the importance of internal learning/rationalism versus experiential learning in an environment/empiricism (Schunk, 2020). Cognitive (internal) perspectives on deeper learning focus on the mental structure of knowledge and the processes of perception, memory, and so on. Sociocultural (external) learning centers around learners participating in their community and using experience in varied settings to learn (National Research Council, U.S., 2012), which is a vivid example of DBI. The chapter states that science, for example, is a sociocultural discipline: it consists of an established community with shared practices where members of the community come together to create and discover or understand, and then revise, through social processes (Polanyi, 1958, as cited by National Research Council, U.S., 2012). This description is quite similar to disciplines typically associated with the Arts and Humanities (e.g., people collaborating to create a movie) and is reminiscent of the work of applied theatre.

Inversely, educational theatre could be said to use science-based teaching methods to instruct. History or English Literature students, for example, may be asked to get up on their feet and participate in group "experiments" such as process dramas so that the classroom more resembles a chemistry lab than a direct lecture course. In fact, the editors note that deeper learning is defined "not as a product but processing" (National Research Council, U.S., 2012) which is what process drama focuses on: the process rather than the end product. When engaged in a sociocultural (e.g., educational theatre) method of teaching, students may, for example, take on the "Mantle of the Expert" (Heathcote & Herbert, 1985) or rather, be surrounded by the conditions in which knowledge and understanding may grow from within and around the student (Aitken, 2013).

Further, the editors (National Research Council, U.S., 2012) discuss cognitive architecture and reinforce the neuroscience explanation of learning: stimuli, working memory, and long-term memory. Their description of problem-solving procedures, the relationship to weak vs. strong methods, and the recall of relevant knowledge is helpful especially in the context of how learning occurs along with understanding the influence of schematic knowledge. The editors go on to note that the thinking of experts versus that of novices can help guide instruction (*ibid.*). Again, this recalls the DBI method described in Heathcote's seminal work regarding the Mantle of the Expert. She posits that the teacher empowers students with the expertise required and then enables them, from within the group, to construct knowledge (Heathcote & Herbert, 1985). This may conflict with the National Research Council, U.S.'s (2012) stance that experts' long-term memory is an important factor in being able to recall and use knowledge, organized in schemas, that can be applied to solving new problems. As a teaching strategy, though, Heathcote uses the Mantle of the Expert to allow students a shift in attitude so that they may work together via a loosely scripted process drama to discover knowledge, reminiscent of the rationalism illustrated by Schunk (2020).

Facilitating a process drama requires skillful leadership by the teacher (who presumably is an expert in the subject and essentially serves as the organized long-term memory bank for the learners to access), and does put the students in an environment specifically crafted to affect their behavior (Heathcote & Herbert, 1985). This is similar to the empiricist approach described by Schunk (2020). The National Academy of Sciences, though, points out that true expertise comes from guided, sustained practice, focus, the incorporation of productive feedback, and the acquisition of cognitive skill over time

(National Research Council, U.S., 2012). Aitken (2013) argues, though, that the Mantle of the Expert technique positions students as competent in the creation of knowledge by placing them in the center of the inquiry. This student-led inquiry creates the framework in which the participants do become "experts" *within the enterprise the teacher has constructed with them*. In this sense, the Mantle of the Expert does not conflict with the National Research Council's point of view, and allows for reflection and even metacognitive learning about the topic at hand (Aitken, 2013).

The editors also mention the Anderson update of Bloom's taxonomy; the update added facts and concepts, procedures and strategies, and beliefs. For knowledge to be deep, or transferable, these updates must be integrated, structural, automated, strategic, and productive on the part of the learner. After practice and the incorporation of useful feedback, the knowledge should become embedded in the learner (National Research Council, U.S., 2012). This is where Heathcote's approach may be said to diverge, but the tactic does create an environment and new expectation for *how* students learn, reason, and develop cognitive skills (Heathcote & Herbert, 1985), thus laying the groundwork even if they are not yet experts. The editors (2012) provide an example of how deeper learning can lead to 21st century competencies and describe the techniques used in implementing a new culture where they assign roles to students as well as empower them with responsibilities including working together to reason and solve problems as well as apply what they are learning (*ibid.*), features commonly seen in process drama (Heathcote & Herbert, 1985). The findings of the example provided show how deeper learning helps the students acquire and transfer knowledge (National Research Council, U.S., 2012).

Deep learning also allows for the *intrapersonal* domain to build 21st century competencies such as work ethic, belief in self, initiative, adaptability, and self-motivation. When students are aware of their learning abilities and understand learning strategies they can employ, they can persist in the face of doubt or unfamiliarity. By self-regulating and being an active learner, students can take part in setting goals with purpose. Self-regulation is, however, difficult to assess. The *interpersonal* domain is also important for building competencies. Teamwork, leadership, collaboration, and the ability to influence are all abilities that students must learn along with course content. Indeed, self-regulation should allow for students to seek social relationships that can help them learn. Understanding deep learning and the concept of knowledge transfer and recognizing the intrapersonal and interpersonal aspects of learning should allow teachers to better construct strategies for instruction (National Research Council, U.S., 2012). The editors (*ibid.*) note that the main challenge is to "create learning experiences for learners that will prime appropriate cognitive processing during learning without overloading the learner's information processing system" (p. 98). When properly facilitated, a strategy such as Mantle of the Expert (Heathcote & Herbert, 1985) is an effective choice and the goal of deep learning may better be achieved (Aitken, 2013; Selderslaghs, 2019). Regardless of teaching strategy, the goal of deep learning and transfer in order to achieve 21$^{st}$ century competencies is essential (National Research Council, U.S., 2012).

## APPLYING LEARNING THEORIES AND INSTRUCTIONAL DESIGN MODELS FOR EFFECTIVE INSTRUCTION

Khalil and Elkhider focus on application of theory and begin with an explanation of the science of how people learn. They cover the same three types of memory as Schunk (sensory, working, and long-term memory) that work together to facilitate learning. Khalil ad Elkhider describe two types of rehearsal: maintenance and elaborative which are alternate terms for surface and deep learning. Whereas maintenance rehearsal is rote memorization, elaborative rehearsal happens when the learner organizes information to create meaning (Khalil & Elkhider, 2016; Schunk, 2020).

When learning theories are correctly applied by teachers via instructional strategies, the goal is deep understanding rather than surface learning. The authors note that learners also employ strategies for organizing, remembering, thinking, self-regulating attitude, and self-motivation which all contribute to learning deeply (Khalil & Elkhider, 2016). One specific example of the difference between verbal information and intellectual skills of particular interest reflects on students' ability to learn and perform process(es). This example was that, "to recall the definition of creatinine clearance is verbal information; however, using the Cockcroft-Gault equation to estimate creatinine clearance to assess the function of the kidneys is an intellectual skill" (Khalil & Elkhider, 2016, p. 148). This is not unlike an actor learning lines by rote versus analyzing the words they are saying for their meaning. Additionally, this relates to participants in an applied theatre lesson being led through a process to construct meaning rather than simply memorizing facts. Because this article is centered in higher education, the authors also cover andragogy and note that adult learners are more likely to be independent and possess more life experience, motivation, and goal-setting ability, and so can better understand how to apply knowledge to a problem (*ibid.*). Younger students in the DBI context, though, will actively and collaboratively participate in knowledge creation with the leader positioning them as stakeholders with a sense of ownership and internal motivation (Selderslaghs, 2019).

In moving towards praxis and applying theory to instructional design and, of course, teaching, Khalil and Elkhider posit five principles of instruction:

- Learners are engaged in solving real-world problems.
- Existing knowledge is activated as a foundation for new knowledge.
- New knowledge is demonstrated to the learner.
- New knowledge is applied by the learner, and
- New knowledge is integrated into the learner's world.
(Khalil & Elkhider, 2016)

This reinforces what the National Research Council chapter covered regarding transfer of learned knowledge to solving novel problems (National Research Council, U.S., 2012). As DBI educators attempt to design and deliver teaching strategies, Khalil and Elkhider note they must situate instruction in real-world, relevant tasks (2016) which is something that Mantle of the Expert is clearly well-suited to do (Aitken, 2013; Selderslaghs, 2019). Furthermore, teachers should be careful not to overwhelm students with little foundation coming into a lesson and should also provide actionable feedback (notably both points were also stressed in the National Research Council chapter) which, again, Mantle of the Expert is appropriate for (Aitken, 2013; Selderslaghs, 2019).

Khalil & Elkhider (2016) go on to discuss the importance of analysis, design, development, implementation, and evaluation in instructional models which recall the iterative plan -> do -> study -> act cycles of continuous improvement (Bryk et al., 2015). In order to combine theory and design and actively apply practical strategies in the DBI classroom, the authors propose a framework for implementation. In the analysis phase, teachers must assess their students' current knowledge, skills, and behaviors so that they know from where they are starting. In the design phase, teachers should craft concrete learning objectives, outline expectations, and determine how they will assess whether students met the objectives in measurable ways. The development phase requires creating the actual content to be delivered to students (e.g., creating the script for a process drama) and preparing the learning environment whether it be a physical space or completely online. The implementation phase is the active teaching and learning during the course. Finally, the evaluation phase is not only the last or summative assessment at the end of the course, but includes formative assessment during each of the other phases. For both kinds of assessment, providing constructive, actionable feedback during DBI is critical for deep learning for both students and educators/instructional designers. Indeed, competency in instructional design by DBI teachers is key for the practical application of learning theory for improved student outcomes (Khalil & Elkhider, 2016).

## TEACHING FOR DEEP LEARNING

Smith and Colby's 2007 study highlighting the correlation between surface teaching and surface learning discusses implications of how to teach for deep learning. Shifting towards looking at teaching theories and strategies rather than learning theories, the authors (*ibid.*) point out that teaching for standardized tests can limit students to surface learning, and that when teachers purposefully teach for deep learning, it is more apt to happen. The study they conducted showed that 64% of teachers were instructing in a way that led to surface learning. Smith and Colby (*ibid.*) note that when teaching strategies call for deeper reflection from students rather than rote memorization, learners will construct more meaning. If students do not naturally possess this ability, teaching strategies such as modeling can help prompt students to process concepts and form beliefs about what they are learning (*ibid.*). Taken even further by the teacher employing DBI strategies, deep, reflective inquiry rather than rote memorization on the part of the student, along with the tensions provided by the facilitator in the process drama setup, allows the student to safely explore real-world situations and solutions (Aitken, 2013).

Assessment as a learning and teaching tool for both students and teachers is also a tactic that DBI instructors can benefit from. Pennison (2004) states that self-assessment is essential to learning, noting that thinking, reflection, interest, processing of information, reaching conclusions, and devising solutions and the application of the same allow students to validate what they are learning for themselves (Dewey, 1916, as cited by Pennison, 2004.) Smith and Colby propose the Structure of Observed Learning Outcome, or SOLO taxonomy, as a way to assess both teaching and learning outcomes (Smith & Colby, 2007). For Pennison, the use of rubrics led to conferences with *students* to discuss ways the student could engage more in learning, and which also led Pennison to reflect on her teaching (Pennison, 2004). Smith and Colby promote collaboration with fellow *teachers* in the use of the SOLO taxonomy to discuss what deep learning looks like, and how as DBI instructors they can support students reaching the next level of the SOLO taxonomy. Because it is a continuum of learning, from missing the point, to two levels of surface learning, and then to two levels of deep learning, the teacher can employ the taxonomy developed by Biggs (1987) to move students from one level to the next rather than simply to assess where they are. Additionally, students can use it to better understand their own approach to learning. As DBI instructors reflect on their instructional design, the SOLO taxonomy and its five levels of learning is an applicable framework for creating rubrics for evaluation (such as those created by Pennison). When those with a stake in teaching and learning realize the value in evaluation for the purpose of examining *how* a student learns rather than *what* a student learns, teaching approaches can be designed to better facilitate deep learning (Smith & Colby, 2007).

## PURSUING THE DEPTHS OF KNOWLEDGE

Boyles (2016) touches on the difference between recall and thinking/reasoning in deep learning. She also gives specific, real-life examples of how assessment relates to instructional planning, moving even further into application of theory in practice. Boyles also discusses the rigor required for both the teacher and the student in her examples. She begins the article by mentioning "teaching for the test" and aligning assessment so that teachers can teach with rigor and students can take an active role in holding themselves accountable as well (Boyles, 2016). Education practitioners have been concerned about teaching to the test for decades. For example, an article from over thirty years ago advocates that teachers and other stakeholders come together to design standardized tests explicitly so that they know the contents are what *should* be assessed; then, they would *want* to teach to the test and know whether students are meeting standards to which instructors think they *ought* to be held. (Wiggins, 1991). Boyles asks what these standards or depth of knowledge should look like, much as Smith and Colby did when they called for teachers to collaborate on this very topic (Boyles, 2016; Smith & Colby, 2007). Boyles also mentions Bloom's taxonomy (as did the Khalil and Elkhider article) but states that it does have shortcomings and goes on to propose four levels of depth of knowledge (Boyles, 2016). These four levels are somewhat analogous to the levels in the SOLO taxonomy in the Smith and Colby article, minus the lowest level of "missing the point" (Smith & Colby, 2007). Boyles contends that these levels are not mutually exclusive, however, and that not only must one build on the other, but the teacher should plan to teach rigorously for each and ensure students know high expectations exist for all levels. In this context, Mantle of the Expert is an excellent method for working with students beyond "teaching for the test." The outcome of a process drama really has no right or wrong answer, it is the process that is important along with the meaning made by the students and teacher. Selderslaghs (2019) gives an example of a process drama about the Titanic, wherein students work out ethical issues, define what it means to be a good citizen, identify actions taken and the motivations for them, inquiring at what costs an action may be taken, and investigating social responsibility. In so doing, these students learned far more than what might be on a standardized test; they learned critical thinking skills and the power of reflective learning (*ibid.*). Students will likely reach most if not all the levels of learning for their context in this use of DBI.

For each level (recall/reproduction, skills/concepts, strategic thinking/reasoning, and extended thinking) Boyles looks at what is required from both teachers and learners to maintain rigor and describes actual, real-life examples that can be transferred or generalized by teachers across subjects in their instructional planning and assessment of student achievement. The fourth level, extended thinking, calls for students to be able to integrate and apply knowledge and skills from more than one source (Boyles, 2016). As an example, modern use of the Socratic method can teach critical thinking rather than simply be employed to discover knowledge (Boghossian, 2006). Or the Mantle of the Expert method (Heathcote & Herbert, 1985) where the facilitator leads students through a dialogue of questions and answers and reasoning to work through an issue or problem may be employed. The end result is not the only goal; the process of arriving to it is just as important. The participants are given responsibilities and must interrogate and think as an expert to learn the topic at hand and come to conclusions through discourse (Heathcote & Herbert, 1985; Roper & Davis, 2000). This is similar to Socratic dialogue in that students will arrive at the truth/knowledge rather than merely accepting what the instructor tells them (Boghossian, 2006; Roper & Davis, 2000).

## THE DEPTH OF KNOWLEDGE: SURFACE, SHALLOW, OR DEEP?

Bennet and Bennet (2008) look at the resulting knowledge once teaching theory, learning theory, and instructional design have been distilled into practice by teachers and students have "learned" something. Bennet and Bennet ask: once someone has learned or acquired knowledge, how does the level of knowledge impact how the person then takes action? Solves problems? Makes decisions? They examine knowledge theory and how depth of knowledge translate into action and the ability of the learner to apply knowledge to other situations (*ibid.*). While this brings us full circle back to the concepts of learning as surface, deep, and achieving (Biggs, 1987) and the idea of "transfer" (National Research Council, U.S., 2012), Bennet and Bennet move beyond educational praxis and discuss implications for deep learning in an individual's life beyond the classroom. The authors discuss the idea of knowledge as patterns of information that exist in the brain that must be interpreted in order to make meaning (Bennet & Bennet, 2008; Schunk, 2020). They *functionally* define knowledge as the ability to act situationally, explicit knowledge as that which a person can recall and express to another, implicit knowledge as that which is accessed when triggered, and tacit knowledge as that which is the understanding of what action needs to be taken but which cannot be transferred to another; tacit knowledge, moving from simply learning to reasoning out how to take action, must be created by each individual (Bennet & Bennet, 2008).

Bennet and Bennet explain surface, shallow, and deep knowledge as well. Surface knowledge answers who, what, where, and when, and is explicit knowledge requiring little or no action. They define shallow knowledge as essentially surface knowledge along with some understanding due to context. This may require or result in action to a certain extent. Deep knowledge is when an individual can take information and truly make meaning, think through it, synthesize it with other information, and know when and how to act through reasoning. Deep knowledge is akin to expertise and requires practice (Bennet & Bennet, 2008). This may be where the Mantle of the Expert, as a teaching strategy, sets the expectation for the learner that they are to *think* like an expert, and should use reason and cognitive skills as an expert would in order to grow, reach conclusions, solve problems, and determine a plan of action in the safe environment of the classroom (Heathcote & Herbert, 1985).

Bennet and Bennet (2008) also provide a taxonomy of knowledge related to taking action, wherein they discuss meta-, learning-, strategic-, research-, praxis-, action-, and description- knowledge categories. These categories can sometimes overlap but understanding the role each category plays is helpful in knowing how a person may apply learning and take action, especially outside the classroom in a real-world environment. Because this article is centered on how knowledge is applied in, for example, the business world rather than assessing whether a student has been able to apply knowledge in a classroom setting, the authors have characterized applied learning in organizational levels with a hierarchy in mind: ontological for higher (executive) authorities who make decisions with the deepest level of knowledge, strategic for management leadership level authorities who make decisions still with a need for deep knowledge, operational for supervisory level authorities who make decisions with a more shallow level of knowledge, and tactical for those with routines requiring only surface level knowledge. The complexity of an organization would also impact the level of knowledge required to understand how to apply learning for the sake of effective action (*ibid.*). Not unlike Bryk's call to see the system that produces the outcome we are getting (Bryk et al., 2015), Bennet and Bennet propose to tackle the organization's structure for operational change through deep knowledge and the ability to transfer such knowledge into reasonable action for a new outcome. Through the analysis of knowledge and of the organization as well as identifying cause, the best actions to take can be recognized and organizational improvement can be realized (Bennet & Bennet, 2008).

## CONCLUSION

The literature takes the reader on a journey from Bigg's seminal piece on the nature of how students learn, replete with learning theory and teaching theory, through discussions about transferring knowledge to novel situations, applying theories to instructional design, applying those designs in the DBI classroom, keeping in mind that how we teach greatly affects how our students learn, and how they then go on in life with the ability to learn on a spectrum from surface to deep. Boyles' discussion about expectations and the rigor required of both the student and the teacher help to synthesize the previous articles and arrive at a place of deeper learning about the topic of this paper. While the Bennet and Bennet article was somewhat esoteric in nature, it provides a view of how people apply learning/knowledge beyond the classroom in an organizational setting. Coming to a deeper understanding of surface versus keep knowledge is a vital tool in the DBI education practitioner/researcher's toolkit for evaluating problems of practice and arriving at a praxis of iterative improvement.

## SUGGESTED CITATION

Burton, B. (2024). Praxis: The application of teaching and deep learning strategies for the DBI education practitioner/researcher. *ArtsPraxis, 11* (1), pp. 140-150.

## REFERENCES

Aitken, V. (2013). Chapter Three: Dorothy Heathcote's Mantle of the

Expert approach to teaching and learning: A brief introduction. In *Connecting Curriculum, Linking Learning,* pp. 34–56. NZCER Press.

Bennet, D., & Bennet, A. (2008). The depth of knowledge: Surface, shallow or deep? *VINE, 38* (4), pp. 405–420.

Biggs, J. B. (1987). Student approaches to learning and studying (1. publ). Australian Council for Educational Research.

Boghossian, P. (2006). Behaviorism, constructivism, and Socratic pedagogy. *Educational Philosophy and Theory, 38* (6), pp. 713–722.

Boyles, N. (2016). Pursuing the depths of knowledge. *Educational Leadership, 74* (2), pp. 46–50.

Bryk, A. S., Gomez, L. M., Grunow, A., & LeMahieu, P. G. (2015). *Learning to improve: How America's schools can get better at getting better.* Harvard Education Press.

Cawthon, S. W., Dawson, K., & Ihorn, S. (2011). Activating student engagement through drama-based instruction. *Journal for Learning through the Arts, 7* (1).

Heathcote, D., & Herbert, P. (1985). A drama of learning: Mantle of the expert. *Theory into Practice, 24* (3), pp. 1173-180.

Kauchak, D. P., & Eggen, P. D. (2012). *Learning and teaching: Research-based methods* (6th ed). Pearson.

Khalil, M. K., & Elkhider, I. A. (2016). Applying learning theories and instructional design models for effective instruction. *Advances in Physiology Education, 40* (2), pp. 147–156.

Kyrimi, K., & Tsiaras, A. (2021). Drama in Education as a tool for enhancing self-efficacy in Primary School children. *Drama Research: International Journal of Drama in Education, 12* (1), pp. 1–18.

National Research Council, U.S. (2012). Perspectives on deeper learning. In J. W. Pellegrino & M. L. Hilton (Eds.), *Education for life and work: Developing transferable knowledge and skills in the 21st century,* pp. 69–99. The National Academies Press.

Pennison, M. (2004). From both sides: Assessment benefits for both teacher and student. *ArtsPraxis, 1* (1), pp. 34–61.

Roper, B., & Davis, D. (2000). Howard Gardner: Knowledge, learning and development in drama and arts education. *Research in Drama Education: The Journal of Applied Theatre and Performance, 5* (2), pp. 217–233.

Schunk, D. H. (2020). *Learning theories: An educational perspective* (Eighth Edition). Pearson.

Selderslaghs, B. (2019). Mantle of the expert: The versatility of Dorothy Heathcote's dramatic-inquiry approach to teaching and learning. *The European Conference on Arts & Humanities 2019 Official Conference Proceedings*. The European Conference on Arts & Humanities, Brighton, UK.

Smith, T. W., & Colby, S. A. (2007). Teaching for deep learning. *The Clearing House, 80* (5), pp. 205–210.

Wiggins, G. (1991). Teaching to the (authentic) test. In A. L. Costa (Ed.), *Developing Minds: A Resource Book for Teaching Thinking* (Revised, Vol. 1). Association for Supervision and Curriculum Development.

## AUTHOR BIOGRAPHY

Currently serving graduate students in The School of Nursing at The University of Texas at Tyler, Brenda is in the Doctor of Education program at UT Tyler and earned her Master of Arts in Educational Theatre at NYU. Her work as an Associate Registrar at UT Tyler led her to her current student-centered position where she coordinates placements and manages contracts with healthcare facilities for nursing clinicals. Prior to her time in the Registrar's Office, Brenda was a Coordinator in Tisch School of Arts' Film and TV Program where she facilitated advisement and registration of undergraduate students. Always seeking to improve communication with students, Brenda is researching how to do so with an eye towards improving student outcomes and producing well prepared graduates.

Printed in Great Britain
by Amazon